God Bless You

Joanna Rose Light

Mom,

You always taught me
to turn it over to the Lord
— this taught me how

Peace, Love & Joy

Kathy

1998

Prayer

The Remedy That Always Works

Joanna Rose Light

Peace of Mind Publishing

Library of Congress Catalog Card Number: 97-92474

ISBN:1-891109-36-7

First Edition 1998

Manufactured in the United States of America
For ordering information see the last page of this book or contact

Peace of Mind Publishing
P.O. Box 10354
Phoenix, AZ 85064
1-800-319-9572

This book is dedicated to the Great Spirit, God.

May all who read this book feel the presence of God and be healed in body, mind and spirit.

CONTENTS

Chapter 3
Affirmations: Words that Heal..........41

Chapter 4
The Healing Power of Relaxation.....51

Chapter 5
Listen to Your Body..........57

Chapter 6
Forgiveness: The Heart of Healing..........75

Chapter 7
Letting Go..........99

Chapter 8
Healing Your Relationships..........121

Chapter 9
Finding the Right Healer for You..........149

Chapter 10
The Six-Week Healing Program..........153

ACKNOWLEDGMENTS

Cover art by Alura Westly from the collection of Sarah Jurak. Celestial Guardian Prints are available. Call (602) 996-0612.

Leo Love edited this book several times and helped in countless ways. His generous donations of time, talent and wisdom are deeply appreciated.

Mervin Britton, Jack Friedland, Louisa von Dessau, Elizabeth Krecker, Michelle Chucko, Gary Lodmell, Sue Gonzales, Michael McDowell, James Swedeen and John Adams provided copy editing.

Cover design by Carlos F. Gonzalez and Debra L. Gonzalez. Author photo by Michael Paulson.

Jack Friedland designed and typeset this book.

Don Weldon introduced me to God and gave me abundant assistance and encouragement to share what I'd been given.

Special thanks to Bernie Siegel, Gladys McGarey, Catherine Ponder, Christiane Northrup and Alan Cohen who gave me, a total stranger, help and encouragement.

Rev. Kathryn McDowell, Rebecca Hauck and Alisa Rleigh helped make this book a reality.

My mother, Sarah Huggins, gave me an excellent religious background and taught me to pray.

Disclaimer

This program is not a substitute for appropriate medical care. If you are sick, please consult a physician in addition to reading this book. The author and publisher assume no responsibility or liability for the results any reader experiences.

All of the stories and examples are true. Some names and minor details have been changed to protect the privacy of the individuals involved.

This course is non-denominational. It is suitable for all faiths. All of the different religions of the world worship the same Spirit. Some call it God, some call it Jehovah, some Jesus, some Krishna, some Buddha, etc. I am not a member of any church, sect or religion. I frequent many different temples, churches and synagogues of every faith—and find the same Great Spirit everywhere.

God is not a person. Whenever you are reading about God it is wise to keep in mind that the writer can only use words as symbols. Writers use words that are familiar, such as father, mother, he or she. God is not a he or a she, though we sometimes speak that way. Often I refer to God as my heavenly father or divine mother, but God is not a person like an earthly mother or father. God is spirit. Feel free to substitute your own familiar words in place of the ones I have used.

Introduction

I DON'T BELIEVE IN GOD

I have never for one minute believed in God. In an instant I went from non-believer to knower.

For the first twenty-two years of my life, I had no interest in God. I was raised in a Christian family that went to church every Sunday and said grace before every meal, but I had no personal experience of God. The whole idea was ridiculous to me. Whenever I asked a question, it seemed the answer was always, "You'll only know after you die."

At the age of fourteen, I became so fed up with trying to make sense out of religion that I refused to go to church. I became a true atheist, believing that this universe was just some kind of accident of nature. For many years, I was committed to the idea that when you die you are simply dead, and that's it.

I was unhappily working a nine-to-five office job. The work was dull and the pay was meager. I wanted to make more money, so I quit my job and went into real estate sales. There I was, twenty-two years old, terribly shy, new in town, and knowing nothing about the real estate business. I was scared to death!

By "chance," I saw an ad for a self-hypnosis class. The ad said, "LOSE WEIGHT, STOP SMOKING, IMPROVE SALESMANSHIP AND MUCH MORE." I enrolled in the course, taught by Don Weldon.

Every day I practiced the techniques I was learning in this class. Twice a day I would lie down and slowly think the words of relaxation that helped my whole body let go of tension. Then I told myself, "I am a great salesperson. I am successful. I am making lots of money now."

In less than a month I was given the Salesperson of the Month award. There were more than fifty salespeople in this company—all of them older and more experienced than I. Using the technique of relaxing deeply and affirming the result I wanted, I earned more money my first month in real estate than I'd made the entire year before. My whole life quickly changed. Even more important than the money I was now making, though, was the information I was learning in Don Weldon's classes.

Not that I agreed with everything he said. In fact, I didn't understand most of his teaching at all. He'd say things like, "There's only one Life."

And I'd think, "What is he talking about?" I often thought that he must be crazy, but I was getting such great results that I kept going back to hear more.

When Don spoke of God, I thought, "I'm not interested." But he said, **"If you don't like the word 'God', use the word 'Life' instead. It means the same thing."**

One day I went to see Mr. Weldon for a private session. As usual, he guided me though the progressive relaxation process. I felt completely calm and tranquil. Then he started talking about God. He said, "God is here right now, Joanna. Open your mind and your heart and you can feel the presence of God. Such tenderness and gentleness. Such kindness and great compassion."

My first thought was, "I'm not interested." But as he continued to talk, I thought, "Well, what have I got to lose?" I opened my mind to see if I could feel anything.

Instantly I felt my awareness expanding to include the entire universe. I could see everything in the whole universe. There were strings or beams of light connecting all people. Everyone was so connected to everyone else that I knew I was a part of everyone. Everyone was a part of me. This new experience was natural, peaceful and perfect. There was an absolute knowing that THIS IS REAL. THIS IS THE TRUTH.

When I opened my eyes and looked around the room, I said, "Now I understand everything you've been saying. There is only one Life. You and I are connected. We are not separate at all."

From that day on I've never had a doubt about the existence of God.

For the next thirteen years I studied various healing techniques. Then I finally realized what makes them all work. The goodness of God!

For eight years I worked as a full-time hypnotherapist. During those years I helped hundreds of people heal their bodies, minds, and emotions with self-hypnosis and regression therapy. I also studied numerous hands-on healing techniques, including polarity energy balancing, massage therapy, Reiki, Jin Shin Jyutsu, and Touch for Health, to name a few.

Before using any of these techniques on my clients, I always said a silent prayer asking God to heal the person in whatever way they needed. I was amazed at how many people reported miraculous healing results.

One day it occurred to me that the techniques I was using had nothing to do with healing. It was the Great Spirit that healed these people—and nothing else.

In 1987 I closed my Self-Improvement Center to study and work full-time with Mike Valenzuella, an Aztec Medicine Man. Mike used herbs and hands-on techniques to heal people. He was so successful that he was booked for more than a year in advance, and he saw more than fifty people a day.

Mike often spoke of the Great Spirit, but his main instruction was always, "You can do this healing only if you have no fear."

One morning as I was driving to Mike's clinic, I thought to myself, "I'm not going to be able to heal anyone today." I was full of fear that day because I was in the process of breaking up with a boyfriend. I didn't know what to do, so I sat in my car and prayed, "God, I can't do it today, so You're going to have to heal these people. I can't do anything today, so You're going to have to do it all. Amen."

That day I made no effort to heal the patients myself. I silently asked God to heal them, and put my hands on their bodies. I relaxed and let God do the work. That was the day the most miraculous healings took place.

Mike immediately noticed the difference, and a few weeks later he blessed me as a Medicine Woman.

In 1992 the words "God Will Heal Your Body" came to me in a morning meditation. I had been praying for a way to share with others all that I had learned about healing. In the same instant I received the title, I also knew the outline and structure of a six-week course. Within a few weeks the first class was presented to a dozen students at a church in Scottsdale, Arizona.

The students reported such amazing results that I was compelled to write down their stories. That's how this book began. Not only did health challenges disappear, but difficulties with finances and relationships also cleared up. The same principles that heal the body also work in every area of life.

Here's what a few participants said:

"My shoulder had been in pain for a long time. The healing just happened one day [during the course]. My shoulder is fine now and my life has improved as well."

— Doris G., Tempe, Arizona

"I've lost weight and established a pattern of exercise that works for me."

— Debie F., Scottsdale, Arizona

"I have improved my willingness and ability to let God in. I recommend it to my friends."

— Brian D., Litchfield Park, Arizona

Reader, you will learn from this book exactly how to do the same six-week healing program at home. You will learn to let God's love transform your body, mind, emotions, relationships and your daily life. Read the entire book through from beginning to end. Then begin the six-week healing program in Chapter Ten.

CHAPTER 1

The Healing Power of Prayer

WHEN YOU ASK GOD FOR HELP, HEALING IS INEVITABLE.

At an inter-tribal powwow for Medicine People, a wise old Cherokee Medicine Man spoke. He revealed the most important thing I've ever heard about healing. He said, "Never attempt to heal someone who has not asked for your help. If you do, you are interfering with their free will and giving away your power. However, if someone does ask for your help, then you must do what you can to help them, even if it is just to refer them to someone else."

I think the Great Spirit works by this same rule. God cannot ignore your prayer. When you ask God to help you, God must respond.

Sometimes the problem is healed instantly. It disappears by itself. At other times your higher power will refer you to a doctor or a therapist. After you pray, everything you need will come to you easily. If you need money, it will be provided at the exact time that is best for you. If it is a medicine or an herb that you require, it will come to you. If you need a doctor or a healer, you will be guided to the right person. Everything you need to restore your peace of mind and health will come to you quickly and easily, but you must first ask God for help, because God will not interfere with your free will.

Free will is the ability to make choices. God, being infinite love, gave you the free will to choose. You are free to keep your problems if you want them. God will not interfere with that choice, but you do have a army of angels who are eager to help you. As soon as you give your consent, heaven and earth move. The act of asking for help sets forces into motion that bring about the perfect solution.

Whatever problem you have, God has a solution for it.

I used to work with a woman named Tammy. She had a health challenge that left her exhausted all the time. She also had financial problems. Her car had been repossessed and her job was about to be terminated. She had neither the energy nor the transportation to look for a new job, so she prayed, "God, I know there must be something out there that will give me the energy I need. Please help me."

A few weeks later a friend gave Tammy a sample of herbal tonic. She tried it and immediately felt that this was the answer to her prayer. She felt so much better that she began to tell everyone about this product. In less than a year she was making more than ten thousand dollars a month from the sale of this tonic. She now glows with health and vitality. Tammy also married the man who invented the product, a multimillionaire.

GOD WILL RESPOND TO YOU

Prayer is communication with God or talking to a higher power. It is a way of mentally joining with a power that is greater than you. There are many different kinds of prayer and there is no wrong way to pray. God will respond to any sincere attempt to communicate with Him.

A young woman named Wendy was terribly sick. She was bulimic and anorexic. Her body had become so out of balance from gaining and losing huge amounts of weight that her doctor told her she had less than six months to live. In desperation she went to an Overeaters Anonymous group and heard about a higher power that could help her. She had no experience of God, but she went outside by herself and looked up at the sky, opened her arms wide, and said out loud, "God, if You're out there, I need help."

She reported, "Immediately I was overwhelmed with a feeling of comfort. I knew there was a higher power that was willing to help me." Wendy not only overcame the disease, but she has since helped hundreds of others to heal their relationship to food.

SCIENTIFIC PROOF THAT PRAYER HEALS

Dr. Randolph C. Byrd, M.D., conducted a ten-month study in 1982 to scientifically determine what effect prayer has on heart patients in a San Francisco coronary care unit. This was the first scientific study of its kind. Dr. Byrd used the most reliable method of scientific testing: a double blind, prospective, randomized protocol. The study included nearly 400 patients. Half the patients were randomly chosen by a computer to receive prayers for healing from prayer groups, while the other patients were not prayed for.

There was no statistical difference between the two groups when the study began. Neither the patients, the staff nor the doctors knew who was in which group. The group who received prayer had less congestive heart failure, required less diuretics and antibiotics, had fewer episodes of pneumonia, fewer cardiac arrests, and needed fewer life support procedures than the control group.

According to Larry Dossey, M.D., writing in the December 1989 issue of *Atlantis, The Imagery News Letter,* "The outcome was so significant that if the method being investigated had been a new drug or surgical technique it would undoubtedly have been heralded as a scientific breakthrough." Commenting on this study, Dr. William Nolen, author of *The Making of a Surgeon,* said perhaps physicians should prescribe "Pray for patient three times a day."

This study is not the only scientific experiment that proves the medicinal effects of prayer. In his book *Healing Words,* Larry Dossey, M.D., states, "A few years ago, I was surprised to discover a single

The Healing Power of Prayer

scientific study that strongly supported the power of prayer in getting well. Because I'd never heard of controlled experiments affirming prayer, I assumed this study stood alone. But did it? Somehow I could not let the matter rest, and I began to probe the scientific literature for further proof of prayer's efficacy. I found an enormous body of evidence: over one hundred experiments exhibiting the criteria of 'good science,' many conducted under stringent laboratory conditions, over half of which showed that prayer brings about significant changes in a variety of living beings. Over time I decided that *not* to employ prayer with my patients was the equivalent of deliberately withholding a potent drug or surgical procedure."

GOD ALWAYS ANSWERS YOUR PRAYERS

A man asked me, "Does God ever say 'No'? It seems that God has not answered my prayer."

I said, "God always answers your prayer but the way that the prayer is answered may not be what you had in mind." Many times we fail to notice that our request has been granted because we expect it to happen in a certain way. There is no way to predict how the results will manifest in your life. It is best to avoid outlining the solution. Just ask God to help you. That is the first step, but as you will see, it may not be the only step.

I know a man who was a hopeless alcoholic. He lost his family and his job as a result of his drinking. Eventually he lost his health as well. One morning he woke up and found that he could not move his body. He was in terrible pain and fear. For the first time he turned to God and asked for help. Immediately he felt better and was able to call Alcoholics Anonymous for assistance. Two men came right over. This started him on the road to recovery. He told me that it wasn't until years later that he realized what a miracle this had been.

We don't always recognize the response of God. Often, it doesn't fit our picture of how healing should look. But our prayers do not go unanswered.

I was bedridden for a year following an automobile collision. Every day I prayed for God to heal me. Nothing happened for a long time. It seemed as if God was not responding to my prayers. I was getting worse instead of better.

Years later I understood why the healing I had requested took so long. I delayed my recovery by failing to follow through with the directions God gave me. Every day when I prayed, God told me what to do. He said in a still, small voice, "Ask your friends for help." I didn't want to ask anyone for help. I wanted God to heal me all by Himself. When I finally did ask my friends for help, I quickly recovered.

How fast your prayer is answered is up to you. If you don't take action when you receive God's guidance, you delay your recovery. God will provide for your healing as fast as you are willing to accept it.

I am convinced that the number one reason for prayers not being answered is that they are never prayed in the first place. We are quick to blame God for our problems but we forget to ask Him for help. Numerous times I've struggled with a problem and thought, "God, why haven't You helped me with this?" Then I realize, I never asked for help. After I pray, the solution comes quickly.

I left a church service one morning. Rain was drenching the parking lot beyond the protective overhang where a man was taking shelter. I said out loud, "O.K., God, please stop the rain for a minute so we can walk to the car."

The gentleman said, "Wow, I never thought to pray for something like that!"

I turned and the rain had stopped. I walked to the car thanking God, but I've never forgotten the look of utter shock on that man's face. We don't think to ask God for a lot of things. We think God is too busy or too important to care about our little needs and desires, but He is not. We don't think of God as something we can really count on in this world—but He is.

God is on your side. He is always willing and able to help you. God is your friend who loves you totally and completely.

Jack, a student of mine, said, "I figured out why my business had been so slow. I forgot to ask God to send me customers. Now I'm praying for paying customers and I'm so busy I need to hire help."

GOD IS YOUR BEST FRIEND

A friend of mine runs a hospital for women who have been sexually abused and those with eating disorders. He wanted me to teach a class for his patients, but he said, "You'll have to change the wording you use. Instead of 'Prayer,' call it something like 'Body Work'."

"Why?" I asked.

He said, "We did a survey of our patients and found that, while most of them believe in God, the relationship is one of fear and guilt. If you use the word 'Prayer' in your course title, it will turn them off."

I said, "That's the real reason they are having problems. Instead of relying on God as their truest friend, they think of God as something to fear. Healing this fear of God is the key to healing their other problems."

So many people think of God as something to fear, but God is the opposite of fear. God is total, unconditional Love. God delights to heal your body and shower you with an abundance of joy, companionship, money and every good thing you desire.

If we fear God, then we will be afraid to ask for His help. We won't pray or meditate and really get to know God personally. Often the fear of God is unconscious. We may not think we are afraid of our Creator, but on an emotional level we feel unwilling to reach out to a higher power. Most individuals have many erroneous ideas about God buried in their subconscious minds.

Your relationship with God is the most important relationship of all. This book will help you feel God's peaceful presence. God is always communicating His Love to you. More than anything, God wants you to remember His Love, and let Him work miracles in your life.

CHAPTER 2

The Healing Power of Love

YOU ARE LOVE

You are not only a physical being. You are eternal life. Your body is alive because the life force of Spirit flows through it. In China this life force is called *chi*. In India it is called *prana*. I call it God's Love. It is God's Love that animates your body. The love that you are is eternal LIFE. When God's Love stops flowing through the body, it is no longer alive, but you are. Your life is not dependent on a physical body. You exist as spirit forever.

YOUR BODY IS ONLY ONE YEAR OLD

Your body is not really as solid as it appears or as old as you think. In one year ninety-eight percent of your body is entirely replaced with new living cells. Five days from now you will have a completely new stomach lining. In five weeks your skin will be composed of new and different cells. In just six weeks you will grow a new liver. Your skeleton, which seems to be solid and rigid, is entirely rebuilt every three months.

Healing is easy because your body is constantly renewing itself. When your body is damaged in any way, it automatically heals itself perfectly because the infinite intelligence of God is flowing through every cell. Mending the body is effortless. Your body has a natural tendency to repair itself because health is the natural condition of life.

PAIN INDICATES WHERE YOU'VE STOPPED LOVING YOURSELF

A man went to his physician and said, "Doctor, my right knee hurts."

The doctor said, "Oh, you're just getting old."

The man said, "Well, my left knee is just as old, and it doesn't hurt."

It is normal and natural to be healthy regardless of how old you are. Contrary to popular belief, it is not natural to experience pain just because you have lived a certain number of years.

When you experience disease, it is because you've lost your awareness of Love's presence. You've forgotten your oneness with Life. God does not make you sick. God's will for you is complete joy, including health, prosperity and peace of mind. When you are unhealthy it is because you are blocking the flow of life somehow. Health has not deserted you. You have abandoned it. Physical problems always have something to do with the flow of love in your life. Somehow you've stopped loving.

David told me his right hand was hurting. He thought it was due to his work. He was a carpenter and he explained that the hammering he was doing every day had caused this pain.

"How long have you been a carpenter?" I asked.

"All my life. I've done the same work for more than thirty-five years," he answered.

"How long has your hand been bothering you?" I questioned.

"It started hurting about a year ago," he replied.

"Well," I said, "I don't think your work is causing the pain. You've been doing the same work all your life. It shouldn't be any different now."

He was silent.

I said, "I was reading a book the other day about the symbology of the body. It said that the right hand is symbolic of giving. My guess is that you are not giving something that you should be sharing."

He said he would think about it.

I saw him a week later. He said, "My hand doesn't hurt anymore. I thought about what I wasn't giving and I knew it was love. The pain started about the same time I got divorced last year. Since then I've not been able to really open up with a woman. I say 'come closer,' but when they do, I push them away."

Life, Love and God are the same. When love is stagnant in your life, the body becomes lifeless. Your body is like a perfect machine that sometimes becomes unplugged. The machine is fine, but it won't work without electricity. Love is the electricity of Life, and the very reason for living. The life energy, or life force, is Love. It is this life force that keeps your body alive. If you stop the flow of love in your life for any reason, your body will tell you about it in the language of pain.

Pain is not punishment from God. God never, ever punishes because God is Love. Pain is simply an indication that you have forgotten your purpose. **The purpose of life is sharing God's Love.** Without love, life has no meaning. Many people lose their purpose because they've forgotten how to love.

The real cause of physical problems is always a decision you made to stop loving. Don Weldon used to tell me that ninety-eight percent of all disease is psychosomatic. After counseling thousands of people in the last seventeen years I see that, not only was he right but that the statement is true for the other two percent as well! Psychosomatic illness does not mean that the problem is all in your head. It means that the *cause* is in your mind. Somehow you've decided that you or someone else doesn't deserve love.

Imagine that the life force, the energy that keeps you alive, flows down from the sky and enters your body through the top of your head. This energy flows through your brain and manifests in your body according to the thoughts and beliefs in your mind. This applies not just to your conscious thoughts, but also to the decisions and beliefs that you are unaware of. Unloving thoughts cause a block in the flow of love, like a clog in the plumbing. The life force can't flow as fully and freely as it was meant to.

A few months after I experienced my first conscious connection with God (described in the introduction), my gynecologist informed me that my pap test was abnormal. Surgery would be required in order to prevent cancer. That was terrifying news. I was twenty-two years old and had already had this surgery twice before. Because I had been studying hypnotherapy, I knew that something in my mind had to be causing this problem to recur. So I went for another private session. I explained the situation to Mr. Weldon and he suggested regressive therapy. In order to prepare my mind, he made a relaxation tape for me that I listened to for a week. During that week, I kept thinking about what might be causing the problem, but I couldn't come up with an answer.

When I went back for the regression I still didn't have a clue as to why my body kept producing abnormal cells on my cervix. But as soon as I was guided into the deep relaxation and told to return to the cause, I knew exactly what was causing the problem.

I remembered a whole string of sexual experiences I had between the ages of six and nine years old. I'd tried to forget this part of my childhood. I had never told anyone about it. I even lied to my husband, telling him he was the first. I had terrible feelings of shame and guilt about my sexuality. I cried for a long time that day and released all the bad feelings. Then I felt better.

I had the surgery and this time it was completely successful. I've never had another problem with that part of my body. This experience taught me an important principle for healing the body: the body always indicates where the emotional problem is. It was no accident that a disease of the sexual organs was caused by guilt and shame concerning sexual experiences.

THERE IS NO PROBLEM THAT LOVE WILL NOT CURE

When you allow more love into your life you let healing into your body. At times we can't see our unloving habits and we don't notice that there is a problem until our body demands that something be done. That is why I say all physical problems are really blessings in disguise. Physical ailments are a message that we need to allow more love into our lives.

Fran came to me for therapy. She was wearing a neck brace because she'd been in an automobile collision and her neck was stiff. I told her, "This is really a blessing in disguise. You'll be grateful that this happened one day soon." I explained, "Nothing happens by accident. Everything happens for your greater good. Sometimes we create pain to slow ourselves down. It forces us to take a look at our life and get on the right track." She came for therapy for several months. During that time, she quit her job as a bookkeeper and got a job as a counselor at a boys' prison. She loved her new job and her new life so much that she phoned me to say, "You know, when you told me that accident was a blessing in disguise, I thought you were nuts! But you were right!"

She needed to love more. Her children had recently left home and her life was empty. She loved her new job because she loved the boys. She knew what she needed and wanted before the collision, but it took the pain to make her take action and apply for the job she wanted.

LOVE MUST FLOW

There must be a flow of love in your life if you want to be healthy. Some people need to give more love, while others must learn to receive it. If there is a block in either direction, your health can suffer.

Receiving and giving love is as natural as breathing. You take air in and then you let it out. The circulation of love is what life is all about. By taking in love and then passing it on to others, you are part of the grand love story that we call LIFE.

Love and life are constantly given to you by God but you must receive them, accept them and pass them on. Love has to flow out from you in order to make room to receive more. If you stop giving love you cannot receive it and life becomes stagnant. Without a healthy flow of love, the body withers.

God is the only source of love. This is important to keep in mind. There is no love but God's Love. When you receive love from others, it is God's Love you are receiving. God's Love comes from Spirit. People pass it around and share it. This is the game of life. Everything else is just make believe. Love is the real business of living.

There are many ways that we interrupt the flow. One of the ways we inhibit the flow is by thinking that love comes from other people. It doesn't. The flow of love in your life is not dependent on how others treat you. It is much more a matter of how you treat yourself.

LOVE YOURSELF

Acceptance is another word for love. Self-acceptance is an essential ingredient for a healthy life. A way to receive more love into your life is to accept yourself as you are right now.

Loving yourself is the only way to get yourself out of a bad situation. If you are feeling terrible, love yourself for feeling terrible. Everyone can benefit from learning to love themselves more.

Love is acceptance. When you stop resisting the way you are and accept yourself, faults and all, healing begins.

Love is a decision. To love yourself is a decision only you can make. You always have the choice to accept and love yourself or to criticize and condemn yourself. No matter what happens, you are free to interpret events in a way that is kind to yourself or cruel. No one else has this power.

No other human being has the power to make you feel like anything less than the perfect child of God that you are. Other people may make unkind remarks but these do not matter at all unless you agree with the opinions expressed by others. A man I was dating once told me, "You're getting too fat." I was hurt and upset by his words until I thought about this question. Why am I really upset? When I honestly examined my mind and emotions, I saw why I was upset by his remarks. It had nothing to do with him. I was upset because I thought I was too fat. It was my own judgment that hurt.

Other people only reflect back to us what we already think about ourselves. Whenever you feel upset about something someone else said, you can be certain that they are mirroring a thought about you that you already believe to be true. *If you didn't believe it, you wouldn't be upset.* This doesn't mean the belief is true, only that you think it is true.

No matter what happens to you, you have the choice of accepting and loving yourself or not. There is no shortage of love. God's Love is always flowing to you in great abundance. But you can limit your awareness of love's presence with your unloving thoughts.

When I was growing up I thought I was ugly. Many people told me that I was pretty but I didn't believe them. Their words had no power to alter my opinion of myself. It wasn't until I started telling myself, "I love and approve of myself," that I began to feel beautiful.

Love is always being offered to you, but it is your choice whether you let it in or reject it. No one can say enough sweet words to make you feel loved if you don't love yourself. No one else can do enough nice things for you to make you love yourself. It is your own thoughts about yourself that matter most. Nobody else can convince you that you are lovable until you decide to accept yourself as lovable just the way you are.

Adam had been suffering from constant pain in his back for many years. He tried medication, physical therapy and even surgery, but nothing helped. After five weeks of attending the God Will Heal Your Body classes he said his back was perfectly normal. Adam shared, "I used to think that people didn't like me, but during your talk about Love, I realized the truth. I didn't love myself. So I started loving and accepting myself and the pain disappeared."

Do you feel unloved? If so, it is not because others don't love you. It is because you don't love yourself. We want others to love us because we don't love ourselves. We want someone else to cherish us, but they can never do it to our satisfaction because love is an inside job. Much more so than romance, love is a do-it-yourself project.

Whenever you accept and love yourself, you will find that other people accept and love you too. As you learn to love yourself more, you will be more aware of the love that others feel for you.

EXAMINE YOUR BELIEFS

I am told that in Australia when a child really wants to insult another kid he says, "You really love yourself." What could a kid say in response to that? "No, I don't. I hate myself!"?

Most children are told some pretty painful things about how they should relate to themselves. As babies we naturally loved everything about us. Then we were taught that it is wrong to love ourselves. The people around us who had forgotten how to love themselves may have communicated that it is selfish or bad to think well of ourselves.

As a child, were you told:

"Don't be selfish."
"Don't brag."
"Only babies cry."
"Love others but don't think too highly of yourself."
"You are only lovable when you behave the way I want you to."
"People won't love you if ...."
"You're too little, too skinny, too fat, too clumsy, too dumb, or too ....?"

Gary, who taught his children to love themselves, told me this story. "When Ben was about three and a half, he was playing with his toys in the corner of my Sedona home. I happened to glance in his direction from the back patio where I was sitting. I saw him sit back on his haunches, take a deep breath and say out loud, 'I think

I'll give myself a kiss.' With that he raised the back of his hand to his lips and gave it a resounding smack. That obvious love of self is quite evident now that Ben is in his mid-twenties and has been blessed with health, athletic and academic success in college and now genuine success and personal fulfillment in his career."

Children tend to believe what they are told repeatedly. If you were told as a child to put other people's needs and feelings before your own, then you probably believe that is the right way to live your life. As an adult you have the freedom and the power to examine the things you were told and to decide for yourself whether or not they work for you now. You can change your behaviors and your beliefs.

I noticed that one of the ways I was unkind to myself was in refusing to take medication. I had read and heard repeatedly that drugs don't cure illness. They only mask the symptoms and make the body toxic. So I decided I'd never take drugs. I stubbornly suffered needless pain because of this belief. Now I believe that pain-relieving medicine, used in moderation, is a act of self love.

Sally shared, "My mother told me I should take care of my husband first, then my children and, if there's any time left, take care of myself. So I never even took a bath because I thought it was wrong to take time for myself just to relax. Now I tell my husband, 'I'm going to relax for thirty minutes, so don't disturb me.' This was hard at first but now I'm changing a lot of my old beliefs and I'm taking the time to love myself."

I had an experience that changed the way I relate to myself. When I was in my twenties I was romantically involved with a man who was unkind to me (the same one who said I was too fat). After an emotionally turbulent year, I broke up with him. A friend told me that she thought he was an alcoholic and that I should go to an Al-Anon meeting. I went to about five of these meetings and the subject we discussed in each one was *acceptance*. I listened to people tell what they thought acceptance was about. Most of them seemed to think that acceptance is an important spiritual quality and that we should accept others as they are, especially the alcoholic.

I don't remember what I said at any of those meetings except the fifth one. Suddenly I realized that the first person I must learn to accept is myself. Acceptance is about loving myself as I am. I decided to put accepting myself before accepting others. A whole new door opened up inside me. I found the freedom to be myself. I didn't have to feel bad about leaving an unhealthy relationship. I suddenly found it easier to express emotions that I couldn't express before because I could now accept myself as I was.

This has been a recurring theme in my life: In order for my own life to work, I have to love myself more than anyone else.

You can only love others if you first accept and love yourself. When you feel good about yourself, then you have plenty of love to give. When you approve of yourself, you will automatically feel love for others.

Love must begin with yourself. Our ideas of what it means to love another person can be pretty mixed up, but if you do what is best for yourself, then you will always do what is best for others.

Shakespeare said it poetically. "This above all: to thine own self be true, and it must follow, as the night the day, thou canst not then be false to any man."

LOVE YOUR BODY

Pauleen said to me, "If only I could cut off this part of my body, I'd feel better."

I said, "If you love that part of your body, you will feel better!"

Love heals. Hate destroys. It is especially important to love the parts of your body that hurt, or look wrong or unattractive to you. The more you love your body, the more lovely your body becomes. Your body needs your love and acceptance.

Sally told me, "I had a huge stomach. Almost every day a stranger would ask me, 'When are you due?' and I wasn't pregnant! I hated my stomach. Nothing I tried made it any smaller until I decided to give it some love. I just started rubbing it and loving it as if it were a little baby. I did this every day and before I knew it my stomach was flat."

Touching your body is a good way to give it love and appreciation. I do this every morning. I start at the top of my head and I lightly touch my hair. I think to myself, "I love and appreciate my beautiful hair." Then I move my hands down over my face and I think, "I love my smooth, clear skin." As I touch my neck, I think, "I love my healthy, strong neck," and so on with each part of my body. This takes less than two minutes to do.

After a seminar, Bonnie said, "I've been touching my body every morning like you showed us and this week has been the first time in years that I could look in the mirror without hating myself."

When you take a bath or shower, give your body love by thinking loving thoughts as you wash yourself. Feed your body with kind thoughts of appreciation. We spend too much time complaining about the things we don't like about our bodies and too little time appreciating the beautiful and healthy parts.

When you appreciate the things about your body that work well, more health is given to you. It is a spiritual law that you get more of what you are grateful for. Remember to thank God for the health that you already have. Gratitude increases health.

I had a problem with a tooth. For about a week nothing helped. Then it finally occurred to me that I had a mouth full of other healthy, perfect teeth. Only one tooth was bothering me. The rest were fine. I thought, "Thank you, God, for all these healthy teeth that serve me so well." Within minutes the problem with the tooth disappeared.

APPRECIATE YOURSELF

To appreciate means to increase in value. Spend some time every day appreciating yourself and your body. It is too easy to find faults in ourselves. Maybe "nobody is perfect," but you must admit that you do have many admirable qualities.

Make a list of at least fifty things you like about yourself and your body. Include talents and skills you possess, personality traits that you are glad you have, and the things about your body that you like. Writing down what you appreciate about yourself will help you focus your mind on your positive qualities.

Making a list of your best qualities is a fun thing to do, but you don't really need any reason at all to love yourself. God loves you unconditionally because you are His child.

Love yourself regardless of how your body looks or feels. Love yourself whether you do all of the assignments in this book or none. You can love yourself whether you have millions of dollars in the bank or just a pile of bills. Your love for yourself can only be limited by you, not by the circumstances that surround you.

Nourish your mind with loving thoughts about yourself. Deliberately think, "I love you!" when you look in the mirror. Tell yourself, "I approve of myself," over and over as you go through your day. Stop criticizing yourself by replacing critical thoughts with loving ones. When you notice a critical thought about yourself, tell yourself, "I love myself unconditionally."

I'M SENDING GOD'S LOVE TO YOU

Sending God's Love is a wonderfully easy way to increase the flow of love in your life. Everyone will do it a little bit differently but, to start, imagine a stream or a beam of God's Love coming down from the sky like a light shining brightly with God's perfect Love. Imagine this light entering your body through the top of your head and illuminating your mind and filling your entire body with God's Love. Imagine that your body is multiplying God's Love like a dynamo. Now send God's Love out through your heart. You can send God's Love to any person, place or situation and it will have a healing effect.

When I first heard about sending God's Love I didn't believe in God. (This was a few weeks before my experience mentioned in the introduction.) But after thinking it over, I decided it couldn't hurt to try it. I had five cats living in my house. I was about ready to take them all to the pound because they had been using my carpet as a litter box for several months. I'd tried everything and nothing helped. I wasn't really expecting much from this process of sending God's Love, either. I thought I'd probably prove to myself that it didn't work.

However, I wanted to give it a fair test, so with my inner voice I spoke. "God, I send Your Love to each cat in this house. I send Your Love into this situation and to myself." Then I went to bed. The next morning I spoke the same words to God even though I didn't believe there was a God. That day was the first time in months that I found no mess to clean up on the floor. They were going outside to do their business. I was thrilled! It was a miracle! The problem was solved.

"Maybe there really is a God," I thought. I continued sending God's Love each day and many more miracles happened. After some practice, I began to feel God's Love and my whole life improved in many tangible ways. My days were easier, my problems were fewer.

Then one day I had a really bad day. I hadn't had a day like that in a long time. Looking back over the day, I realized I'd forgotten to send God's Love ahead of me that morning. It really does make a difference.

If there is a situation in your life that you've tried to improve but nothing worked, try this: speak no words, just send God's Love.

Whatever the problem, love is the answer. Love is the solution to every problem. There is no problem that enough love will not heal.

Two different doctors told Harry, a 64-year-old man, he had only a few weeks to live. He had recently had heart surgery. His body was retaining water and his whole body was swollen. He was weak and scared. I gave him the God Will Heal Your Body tape to listen to every day and I taught his wife and daughter to send God's Love to him every day.

He returned in a week and I hardly recognized him. He had lost twenty-eight pounds. I said, "You look great! What happened?"

He said, "My doctor just happened to remember a drug that has been off the market for eighteen years. My wife called around and found a drug store that still had it. I lost four pounds the first day, ten pounds the next day, ten pounds the third day and four pounds yesterday."

"That's a miracle!" I exclaimed.

His wife said, "We sure were lucky that the doctor happened to remember that medicine."

"Luck had nothing to do with it," I said. "It's the love that you've been sending that caused the doctor to think of the perfect medicine. Remember, all healing comes from God. Give the credit to God."

Now, four years later, Harry is still living an active life.

SEND GOD'S LOVE AHEAD OF YOU

Begin the day by sending God's Love ahead of you, and your whole day will be much more pleasant. Don Weldon said, "Your vibrations go ahead of you. Suppose you wake up late and cranky. Then you cut yourself shaving and burn the toast. You go to work and everything is already turned upside down when you get there. You say, 'I didn't have anything to do with this because it was already a mess when I got here.' But your negative thoughts *did* create the turmoil at work because your thoughts and feelings went ahead of you."

When you send God's Love ahead of you everything flows smoothly. Whatever you need comes to you easily. People respond to you kindly. When you send God's Love in the morning you are sure to have a lovely day.

When I start my day I say, "God, I send Your perfect Love ahead of me into this day. I send Your Love to everyone I will come in contact with today, in person or on the phone. I send Your Love into every communication today. I fill this house to overflowing with Your divine Love so that all who enter here, myself included, will feel your loving Presence. I send Your Love to myself, to my body and into my relationships, my work and my finances. God, I send Your Love out to everyone in this city, this state, this country, and to everyone on earth. I send an extra abundance of Love to all the world leaders. I cover this planet with a huge cloud of God's Love and I send beams of God's Love to each man, woman and child on earth, leaving no one out."

Before I go to sleep, I send God's Love ahead of me into my dreams and into tomorrow. Often I just let God's Love flow out to wherever it's needed.

As you send God's Love out to the world, you not only bless others but you receive a blessing yourself. Whenever you send God's Love, that Love flows through you to help and heal you in any way that you may need.

Now I send God's Love through, around and behind each of these words so that everyone who reads this will feel the truth of Divine

Love. Stop right now and feel God's Love. Such tenderness, gentleness, kindness and great compassion. God's Love is all around you RIGHT NOW.

SEND GOD'S LOVE OFTEN

God's Love will bring peace, harmony and healing to the people and situations you send it into. Your thoughts direct God's Love. You can send Divine Love to one person or a billion just as easily because God's Love is unlimited. You can multiply God's Love by saying, "I send God's Love to Mary Smith and to everyone on earth."

God's Love can be sent labeled or unlabeled. For instance, if I send God's Love to my friend John to help heal his broken arm, then God's Love will heal his broken arm only. But if I send God's Love to John unlabeled, then it *will* help heal his arm but it will also help him in many other ways that he may need.

God's Love is not limited by distance. You can send God's Love to your friends across the globe and they will feel it in some way.

When you send God's Love it is best to think of it as unmotivated goodwill, rather than an attempt to manipulate a situation to your liking. When you let Love have its way the result will always be perfect for everyone involved.

Doug, a man about twenty years old, came to one of my classes. He complained that he had lost his job and did not know what he wanted to do with his life. He was living with his mother. He said they didn't get along very well. I taught him to send God's Love to himself and to his mother. In a few weeks he told me he had remembered how much he enjoyed taking art classes when he was in school and he now knew that he wanted to become a professional artist. He even knew which art school he wanted to attend. The only problem was that he did not have the money to pay for the tuition.

I said, "Just keep affirming that God will provide a way for you to go to art school." The next week he told me that out of the blue his mother had volunteered to pay for his training. He completed school and became a successful graphic designer.

Louie, a man in his late fifties, came to one of my seminars. He had a patch on his right eye, but he said his goal was to heal his broken heart. He was going through a divorce which he did not want. I taught the group how to send God's Love.

At the next meeting he said, "That sending God's Love really works. I went to a dance and I saw a woman sitting across the room. I started sending her God's Love and after a while I asked her for a dance. Then I couldn't get rid of her. She just wanted to talk and dance all night. The same thing happened with two other women." He came to class with a big smile on his face every week after that. His broken heart was healed because he was loving again.

Trisha shared with me that she was in a hospital emergency waiting room in the wee hours of the morning. The only other person in the waiting room was a woman who was sitting way across the room and sobbing. Trisha sat there and sent God's Love across the room to the crying woman. In a few minutes the woman got up and walked over to her with her arms outstretched. They hugged, and the woman thanked Trisha over and over. She had felt the Love that was being sent to her.

As you learn to give and receive more love, you become more aware of the presence of Love and you see it everywhere. I see two kittens curled up together and I think, "There's Love." I see an old couple holding hands as they stroll through the park. I think, "There is Love." I see a mother feeding her child; strangers rushing to the scene of a wrecked car to help; children playing together; a young girl helping a old woman walk. Love is everywhere to be seen, when you look with loving eyes.

SENDING GOD'S LOVE

CHAPTER 3

Affirmations: Words That Heal

Words are a power more awesome than nuclear energy. Words create. The Bible says, "In the beginning was the Word, and the Word was with God, and the Word was God." (John 1:1) Your choice of words when you pray can make the difference between success or disappointment.

Positive words affirm health, negative words affirm disease. To affirm means to make firm, to make real. Words create by making feelings more real. Every word you think creates a mental picture in your mind and evokes feelings. Every thought you think is in fact a prayer. As you will soon see, the way that we pray is often negative. We inadvertently ask for pain when we use negative words.

The Bible says, "whatever you ask for in prayer, believe that you have received it, and it will be yours." (Mark 11:24) The words we use in our prayers reveal whether or not we believe that God has heard us. The prayer technique you will be using is affirmative prayer. You will be repeating a positive affirmation in a calm and relaxed state of mind. This type of prayer works quickly because it helps your mind to accept the idea of health. The following information about wording your affirmations is vitally important.

WRITE THEM FIRST

Always write your affirmations down on paper before you use them in prayer. That way you can look at them and see if they are worded exactly right before you use them.

FOCUS ON THE SOLUTION

Your words will be healing if you speak about the answer, not the problem. For example, let's say you are bothered by allergies every spring, and you want to be free of this problem. How would you word an affirmation to heal this condition? By focusing on the solution. You write the result you want as if you already have it. For example, "I now breathe easily in all seasons and in all circumstances."

What if your problem is migraine headaches? How would you use words to create a feeling of health? You could write something like, "I have no more headaches," but this would not produce the results you want. Why? Because you are thinking about the problem. A statement with the word *headache* focuses your mind on the problem, thereby making it worse.

The answer is to write about the result you want. How do you want to feel? You want to feel well. You want your head to be clear. The statement, "My head is clear and I feel well," will promote healing because it focuses your mind away from the problem and on the solution.

Words invoke feelings. Your body responds to your thoughts and words. If you want to create healthy feelings, then you must choose words that speak of health, energy, life and enthusiasm.

I FEEL GOOD

After you've written your affirmation, check to be sure that you have not used negative words such as NOT, NO, WON'T, CAN'T, DON'T or STOP.

Negative words will produce negative results. Compare the statement: DON'T DRINK AND DRIVE with the statement: STAY SOBER

"Don't drink and drive," is a negative statement because it makes you think about drinking. It can produce a negative result or action because it brings to mind the opposite of what you want. "Stay sober" is positive because it focuses your mind on the solution. Be sure your affirmation is stated in positive terms.

One of my students, Janet, said, "I don't want my ankle to hurt any more. I want the pain to go away."

43

I told her, "That's not saying what you want. You're talking about what you don't want. What do you want?"

"I want my ankle not to hurt!" she insisted.

"How could you say that without using the word 'NOT'?" I asked.

"I don't know," she admitted.

I said, "Look, Janet, I know your ankle has been hurting for years. But if it wasn't hurting, how would it feel?"

"It would feel good," she said hesitantly.

"Yes!" I exclaimed. "You want it to feel GOOD. A powerful affirmation for you would be, 'My ankle feels good now'."

Affirm what you want, not what you don't want. It is best to avoid words such as "pain-free", or "fat-free." These words are negative instructions to your body.

Your words paint a picture in your mind. Your brain then creates the same picture in your personal world. For example, when you want to move your body, how do you do it? First you picture the movement in your mind. Then your brain coordinates all of the different muscles and nerves and your body moves. Normally you do this so quickly that you don't think about it, but everything you experience is first a picture in your mind.

When you use negative words you are painting a vivid scene of what you don't want. It's like painting a huge billboard of what you don't want and then pasting a 3x5 card on the billboard that says "Not this." When you look at the billboard, your mind sees the picture and ignores the small card that says "Not this."

Choose words that paint a picture of what you *do want*. Fill your mind with words of health, improvement and recovery. When you think or speak of radiant health and harmony, your mind creates a picture, and your body automatically begins to express the idea of radiant health and harmony.

I AM HEALTHY NOW

Your affirmations should be written in the present tense, as if you already have what you want.

Bob said, "I've been affirming for months that my vision is going to be 20/20, but nothing has improved."

I asked, "When is it going to be 20/20?"

"Soon, I hope," he answered.

I said, "There is no future. Now is the only time that exists. If you want perfect vision, affirm that you have it now. The words 'going to be' mean nothing."

Bob changed his affirmation to, "My vision is now 20/20." At the end of the six-week course, he reported that he'd had his eyes checked and they were indeed 20/20. He said, "I got my driver's license changed so that I am not required to wear glasses for driving anymore."

One of the most powerful words you can use in your affirmations is NOW.

Richard, a man in his sixties, was receiving chemotherapy treatments for cancer. He said, "Are you saying I'm supposed to tell myself 'I am healthy,' even though it's not true?"

I said, "Yes! Twice a day you are going to relax your body and your mind and affirm that what you want is true now. This will speed up the healing process tremendously because your body responds to your thoughts. It's as if you are instructing the computer in your brain to heal your body."

"It's hard for me to believe that this is going to do any good," he commented.

I said, "That's exactly why you need to do it. Affirmations correct our negative beliefs. If you really believed you were going to get well, you wouldn't need to affirm health. You would already be completely well. As you tell yourself daily, 'I am now healthy and well,' you will begin to believe it. You will start to expect a fast recovery. This alone will make you feel better, and you will heal much faster."

Richard later reported that his doctor was amazed at the rapid speed of his recovery.

Affirmative prayer does not mean you are to ignore a physical problem and avoid seeking professional help. It is simply a time when you use your imagination and allow yourself to think of the outcome you want. This will give you a positive expectation of successful medical treatment.

"Thank you, God, for my strong, healthy body," is an excellent affirmative prayer. Thanking God before the evidence is visible is a powerful way to increase your faith. You will find that as you daily give thanks for health you will develop unshakable confidence in a successful outcome.

Any affirmation can begin with, "Thank you, God, for_____," or "I give thanks to God that_____." Jesus thanked God *before* he fed over four thousand people with just seven loaves and a few fish. He also gave thanks to God for answering his prayer *before* he raised the dead. If you need a miracle, give thanks to God *before* the results are obvious. Whenever I ask God to heal others I always conclude with, "We thank you, God, that you always answer our prayers. And so it is. Amen."

MAKE YOUR AFFIRMATIONS SHORT AND SIMPLE

Make your affirmation clear and simple. It is best to use small words and short sentences. Your affirmation should be easy for you to remember.

You can use two or three short sentences that relate to one goal. For example, when I wanted to heal a pain in my neck, I wrote, "My neck is healthy and normal. My neck is flexible and strong."

PERSONALIZE YOUR AFFIRMATIONS

An affirmation that includes your name will be more effective than one that doesn't. Customize the affirmations in this book by inserting your name. For example, "I, Joanna, am healthy now," or "I, Joanna, am strong and energetic."

You are not limited to the stock prayers other people write. Now that you know the principles of positive words, you can create your own affirmative prayers. You can now tailor the affirmations to fit you exactly. A woman named Margo said that she wanted to be free of the pain in her side, so she wrote, "My side feels good now."

I said, "That's very powerful. Does the pain bother you at certain times?"

"When I bend down," she answered.

"You could add, 'I, Margo, can bend down with ease now'."

You now have the knowledge to create your own personalized affirmations. Be creative and experiment with different words. Find the words that appeal to you most. For example, if your goal is to reduce your weight, do you want to be thin, slender, skinny, or lean? Choose words that excite your emotions. A statement that clicks for you emotionally will produce the fastest results.

CHECKLIST FOR EFFECTIVE AFFIRMATIONS

1. Write the affirmation down on paper.

2. Check it carefully to be sure that it is positive. Make sure that you are focusing on the answer rather than the problem.

3. Be certain that it is written in the present tense, and add your name.

4. Use small words and short sentences.

WRITE YOUR PERSONAL AFFIRMATION NOW

It is essential that you create an affirmation for yourself and write it down now. You may write it here in this book, or on a separate piece of paper or notebook. In the next chapter, you will be incorporating your personal affirmation with a deep relaxation prayer. You will need to have your written affirmation handy to do that healing process.

My personal affirmation is:

_____

_____

_____

A variety of healing affirmations are located in Appendix A, page 161.

CHAPTER 4

The Healing Power of Relaxation

LEARNING TO RELAX

It is a widely accepted scientific fact that over ninety percent of all illness is caused by stress or tension. This means that the vast majority of physical problems can be healed simply by relaxing and letting go of stress. Deep relaxation is the remedy for stress. Therefore it is an essential part of this healing program. When you relax your body and mind, healing is automatically accelerated.

Ten minutes of deep relaxation provides the restful benefits equivalent to four hours of sleep. The daily practice of deep relaxation will accelerate your healing, increase your energy, enhance your creativity, and improve your ability to concentrate.

The healing power of affirmations is multiplied when the affirmation is thought or heard in a state of deep relaxation. Affirmations are like seeds you plant in your mind. Before a farmer plants a seed, he first prepares the soil. He plows it, loosens it up, and fertilizes the ground. Then when he plants the seed, it will grow and produce food. Using affirmations without deep relaxation is like a farmer who just throws a handful of seeds on the hard dirt and hopes for the best. Some seeds may grow, but you are sure to get a much more successful crop if you take the time to prepare the soil.

Deep relaxation prepares your mind to receive the affirmation. When you relax your body, your brain waves change. These changes can be measured with biofeedback instruments. When your body is relaxed your mind is open to accept new ideas and new possibilities.

For your first experience of deep relaxation, I recommend listening to a tape. My students listen to a tape titled God Will Heal Your Body every day during this six-week program. This tape is professionally produced with original relaxing music in the background. You may order this cassette, or make your own recording of the Healing Relaxation Tape Script in Appendix B, page 169. To order the tape, see the last page of this book.

LISTEN TO YOUR TAPE

Relaxation is something that you must experience. It is not enough to simply read the Healing Relaxation Tape script. Talking about relaxation or reading about it will not give you the healing benefits of actually doing it. Listening to the tape with your eyes closed will help you to achieve a state of deep relaxation quickly. Once you know how it feels to relax completely, you can easily learn to relax without a tape.

PRACTICE RELAXING BY YOURSELF

Tapes are great tools to help you get started, but you will also want to practice deep relaxation on your own, with no tape. There will be times that you may need to relax when there is no tape player handy. If you know how to relax by yourself, then you can use this wonderful skill in any circumstance. Suppose you are on vacation or at work and you get a tension headache. Because you know how to relax, you can sit down, close your eyes for ten minutes, and relax your body and mind. The headache will disappear. You don't need any equipment. All you need is practice.

Learning to relax is easy. It is, in fact, effortless. All you need do is set aside a time to relax. You will need ten minutes to do the relaxation prayer. Practice this process once every day. It usually works best to do this at the same time every day. That way you will easily remember to do it.

Before you begin the process, make sure you will not be interrupted. Turn off your telephone ringer and tell the people you live with that you are not to be disturbed. A DO NOT DISTURB sign on the door is a good idea. Choose a fairly quiet place in which you can focus on relaxing your body and mind.

You may either sit or lie down. If you choose to lie down, stay awake. This is not a time to sleep. You will be relaxing your body and mind much more deeply than you do when you are sleeping. It is common for people to clench their teeth or fists when they are asleep, so they are not physically relaxed. Most folks have more stress and tension than they realize.

The art of relaxation is really the art of doing nothing. Relaxing is effortless. The less you try to relax, the more relaxed you become, so don't try to force yourself to relax. Just *allow* yourself to let go.

THE RELAXATION PRAYER

Read the following script over several times before you begin the relaxation process. It is not necessary to memorize it word for word, but you do need to think in words. Vague concepts are not as effective as specific words. Stay awake as you do this process. Your eyes should be closed. Begin by taking a deep, slow breath in and out. Put all thoughts and cares aside for this time of relaxation. Focus your full attention on your body and your thoughts. Think these words very slowly to yourself.

DEAR GOD, HELP ME TO RELAX MY BODY AND MIND.
MY RIGHT FOOT IS RELAXING NOW. (Allow your foot to relax.)
MY RIGHT LEG IS RELAXING NOW.
MY LEFT FOOT IS RELAXING NOW.
MY LEFT LEG IS RELAXING NOW.
BOTH OF MY LEGS ARE COMPLETELY RELAXED.
MY RIGHT HAND IS RELAXING NOW. (Imagine your hand letting go.)
MY RIGHT ARM IS RELAXING COMPLETELY.
MY LEFT HAND IS RELAXING NOW.

MY LEFT ARM IS RELAXING COMPLETELY.
BOTH OF MY ARMS ARE COMPLETELY RELAXED.
NOW I'M GOING TO RELAX THE REST OF MY BODY BY TAKING THREE DEEP BREATHS. (Take three deep, slow breaths.)
MY NECK AND SHOULDERS ARE RELAXING NOW.
MY SCALP IS RELAXING.
MY FACE IS RELAXING NOW.
MY THROAT IS RELAXED NOW.
(Slowly count backwards from seven to one.)
NOW I AM COMPLETELY RELAXED.
I AM LEARNING TO RELAX MY BODY MORE AND MORE EACH TIME THAT I PRACTICE THIS PROCESS.
GOD IS HEALING MY BODY NOW.
I AM WILLING TO ALLOW GOD TO HEAL ME.
(Repeat your personal affirmation three times to yourself.)
THANK YOU, GOD.
Open your eyes.

THE IMPORTANCE OF REPETITION

Once you get the hang of it, the time you spend in deep relaxation is blissfully pleasant. This Relaxation Prayer takes about ten minutes to do. You are to practice it once each day. It will be well worth your time to develop this skill.

As you learn to relax more and more deeply, you may at times feel a sensation of sinking, floating, tingling or any number of different sensations. Each person's experience is unique, and each relaxation session is different. *What makes deep relaxation healing is repetition.* You may feel very relaxed during one session and not much at all in another. That's O.K. Your feelings or sensations are not nearly as important as the habit of repetition. Keep practicing every day.

My students often say, "I don't have time to relax. I'm too busy."

I tell them, "If you will take the time to do the relaxation prayer, you will be able to get more done in less time. You will think clearer and make fewer mistakes." Without exception, those who try it agree that it works.

CHAPTER 5

Listen to Your Body

YOUR BODY IS WISE

Learning to love your body involves learning to listen to your body. Listening to your body is easy. Your body is screaming loudly for what it needs. You simply have to respond with love to your body's messages.

You have an inner wisdom that will tell you clearly what you need to do in order to be healed. Your body knows what it needs and what it doesn't. Your body knows what is good for it and what is not. Many of us are so used to looking outside ourselves for healing that we are out of touch with our own body. People often ignore the body's messages, abusing or neglecting the physical needs of the body, for years. We are so willing to believe what "the experts" tell us that we don't bother to listen to our own body.

HOW TO LISTEN TO YOUR BODY

Sit down and take three deep slow breaths to relax. Tell your body you will give it whatever it needs. Then just ask the question.

What do you need? The first thought that comes to you is usually correct.

You can also ask, "What do I need to do in order to heal my body?"

One woman said that she asked her body, "What must I do to cure this headache?"

Her body screamed, "GET THOSE PANTYHOSE OFF ME!" She took off the hose and her head felt better right away.

Some find it helpful to touch the part of the body in question. For instance, to put a hand on their stomach before asking, "What do I need to eat?" This process takes less than a minute to do and it is very powerful. When you feel like you need something but you don't know what, take a minute to ask your body, "What do you need?"

When my students learn to listen to their body, they frequently report that they are surprised at what their body needs. Dan said, "I thought I was hungry, but when I asked my body what it needed, it said, 'WATER.' I wasn't really hungry, I was just thirsty." Judy shared, "When I asked, 'What do I need to do to improve my vision?', my body said, 'STOP SMOKING SO MUCH'." You may be surprised at what your body needs.

PAIN IS RESISTANCE

I was massaging Mary Jo's back when she looked up and said, "I have a pain in my back that I've had for years and I would like you to help me release it."

I said, "O.K., I will help you. All pain is resistance. There is something you are afraid to feel. I will help you really be present with this feeling. When you let the sensation be, it will disappear. Where is it located?"

"It's on the left side of my lower back."

"How big is it?" I asked.

"It's about the size of a large mushroom. It's got a cap that sticks out from my body and a stem that is going into my back."

"What texture is it?" I asked.

"It's spongy, like a mushroom. There are little spores like a mushroom has."

"How big is it?" I asked again.

"It's about the size of a silver dollar."

"And what color is it?" I asked.

"It's beige."

I said, "Now I want you to release the past, even the recent past of just a moment ago, and really be in the present. Now, tell me what the sensation in your back is like."

"It's like a mushroom sticking into my back."

"How big is it?" I asked.

"It's smaller, about the size of a quarter," she said with surprise.

"And what color is it?"

"It's beige with black spores," she answered.

"What texture is it now?"

"It's airy, like a mushroom," she said.

"O.K., good," I said. "You're doing fine. Now I want you to release the past. Even a moment ago is the past. Now, I want you to really be in the present time and tell me how your back feels."

"The pain is much smaller now! It's smaller than a penny."

I asked, "What shape is it?"

"It's still a mushroom shape but the stem is very small now."

"Look and see what color it is now."

"It's disappearing as I'm talking. It's gone," she reported. "It's completely gone."

I said, "You stopped resisting it."

We usually try to avoid feeling unpleasant sensations. It is this avoidance, not the sensation, that is painful.

Bless your pain, for it has a divine purpose. Rather than trying to get rid of it, listen to it. What is your pain trying to tell you?

Mary Jo told me later that the mushroom symbolized how she felt. She said, "You know the saying, 'They keep me in the dark and feed me what a mushroom is fed'." Several years later she reported that the pain in her back had never returned.

For more than ten years my neck was my "Achilles' heel." I had been in three automobile collisions and suffered from three different whiplash injuries. There was constant pain. I went for chiropractic adjustments regularly and several doctors who had taken x-rays told me that I'd have to take good care of my neck in order to avoid further deterioration. They said I'd just have to live with this problem for the rest of my life.

It was during the section of the class where I was teaching my students how to listen to their bodies that I finally decided to find out what this pain was trying to tell me. I sat in a chair and took three deep breaths to relax. I listened to the pain. I felt that I should move my head in a way that seemed strange to me but, when I did this, the pain immediately stopped.

I'd been holding my head in the wrong position for more than ten years. Once I felt the correct position, it seemed like I was walking around with my head bowed for a couple of weeks. But this was the correct and normal position. My neck has been perfectly normal and pain free for years now.

When I prepare women for painless childbirth, they give birth with no drugs and no pain. Why? Because they are relaxed and unafraid. It is fear that makes us experience pain. The women of primitive African tribes do not fear childbirth and it's no big deal to them. They deliver the baby easily, put the child on their back and return to work.

American women are taught to fear giving birth, so when the uterine contractions begin, they tighten up in fear. The contractions are painful because the mother is resisting the feeling.

YOU'RE THE EXPERT

No one knows what your body needs better than you. When your body gives you a message, take action. For example, when you feel the urge to use the bathroom, go there immediately. It is common for people to put off these simple needs of the body because they are "too busy." Love your body by making its needs more important than anything else. Nothing is more important than your health.

PHYSICAL NEEDS

Your body has needs. It requires certain things in order to function properly. In our busy world, we forget about the importance of taking care of the body. Some people even use spirituality as an excuse for abusing the body. We hear of spiritual masters who can drink arsenic and not get sick and we think that means we can say a prayer, drink all night and not suffer the consequences of overindulgence. Until you can walk on water, it is wise to care for your body with love and common sense.

There was a woman who was considered by many to be a spiritual saint. However, she was a smoker, and she died of lung cancer. In James Michener's book *Hawaii* there is a scene where missionaries on a long sea voyage suffer from constipation due to lack of exercise. They complain that God allowed them to suffer while the sinning sailors didn't have this problem. The sailors were busy doing physical work all day. They were taking care of the body's need for exercise.

The basic needs of the body are air, food, water, exercise, elimination and rest. Don't expect your spirituality to be a substitute for the physical things your body needs. When you pray for healing, God will send you the help required to take care of your physical needs.

DEEP BREATHING

We take life in through the breath. Your body can live for months without food, and days without water. But you cannot live more than a few minutes without breathing. Nothing gives you energy and clarity of mind like deep breathing.

Take three deep breaths right now. In... and out. In... and out. In... and out.

Don't you feel better?

Most people hold their breath more than they breathe. Elizabeth said, "When I made a point of focusing on breathing deeply, I really began to feel more energy and less stress."

Your day is full of opportunities to breathe life into your body. Remember to breathe deeply as you go about your daily activities. Breathe deeply when you are working. Take deep breaths when you have to wait in line and when you are driving.

It is impossible to feel scared when you are breathing deeply. Whenever you feel afraid remember to take three deep, slow breaths and you will begin to relax.

FOOD

If you read books about nutrition you're likely to become confused. One authority contradicts the other. One year protein diets are in;

the next year carbohydrates are the rage and proteins are considered bad. How can you know who to listen to?

When it comes to your body, you are the best authority. Every body is different. What's good for one person is not good for another. If you listen to your body it will tell you what it needs.

Those who diet a lot tend to get out of touch with their bodies. Their weight goes up and down because they are always trying to eat according to what someone else says. Many don't even know when they are hungry. They eat because it's time to eat or because they are emotionally upset.

Many of my students release pounds during this course. They tell me they are amazed at how easy it is to say "No thank you" to foods which they used to find irresistible. This is what I teach:

1. Listen to your body prior to eating.

2. Bless all food before you eat it. You may simply think, "Thank you, God, for this food," to yourself, or use whatever form of blessing you prefer.

My favorite blessing, which I recite either silently or aloud before I eat is...

Dear God, I thank you for this food. I bless it and fill it with your light and love that it will nourish me and strengthen me physically, mentally, emotionally and spiritually. And so it is. Amen.

Blessing your food is very important. It gives you a moment to relax and be grateful for the food you are about to eat. To bless means to pronounce it good. No matter what you are eating, bless it. Call it good and you body will use it to nourish and strengthen you.

3. When you bless your food, add this prayer: "God, help me to eat only what my body really needs right now."

Ted said, "That prayer really works. I find myself full and satisfied halfway through the meal, so I just save the rest for later. This is a miracle for me." Susan shared, "I can even go to an 'all you can eat' buffet and walk out comfortably satisfied rather than stuffed and miserable."

I believe that no food or drink is inherently bad, but that anything can be abused. Whatever you eat, don't overeat Whatever you drink, do it in moderation. Ask God to help you develop the consciousness of moderation. If you listen to your body, you will never overeat. Your body doesn't like it when you overstuff it. It feels uncomfortable. By listening to your body, you will know when to push the plate away.

4. Think happy thoughts. Cheerful thoughts create chemicals in your body that balance your weight. We tend to think, "I'll be happy when I lose weight" or "When I'm different somehow, then I'll be joyful." That line of thinking is backwards. Life doesn't work that way. When you learn to be happy regardless of your shape or size, then your body will automatically change. Excess

pounds will disappear when you think happy thoughts. One day you'll notice that your clothes are baggy.

Happiness has nothing to do with your circumstances. You can only be happy when you are thinking thoughts that make you feel good. The secret of happiness is profoundly simple. You can choose to be joyful right now. Just think of something that makes you happy.

If you are not glad there can be only one reason. You are thinking unhappy thoughts. If you dwell on sad, scary or depressing ideas, then you will feel sad, frightened or depressed. One student said, "Now I know why I've been so depressed since I had my baby and quit work. I've been watching soap operas all day." She turned off the TV and by the end of the course she had lost eighteen pounds.

LOVE YOUR BODY BY EXERCISING

Your body needs exercise to function properly. The lymphatic, circulatory, digestive, respiratory and muscular systems can't function properly without regular periods of exercise. Your whole body is designed for movement.

Besides my prayer time, I consider exercising to be the most important thing I do. There is no substitute for exercise. If you don't exercise, you will not feel your best. Exercise increases the life force in the body more than anything I know.

I have seen major physical limitations overcome with simple stretching exercises. Norma's neck was so stiff and deformed that she had to sleep with three pillows. I taught her a few gentle stretching exercises and in less than a month her neck was normal. Ed could not raise his arm over his head. I showed him how to stretch the arm and shoulder muscles and before long he had regained full range of motion.

The body responds quickly with increased aliveness when you exercise. Exercise cures mild depression and makes weight control much easier.

Again, seek the spirit of moderation. It doesn't take strenuous exercise to get the benefits. A brisk twenty minute walk, three times a week is all that is necessary. Choose an exercise program that is enjoyable for you and don't overdo it. Start slow and easy. If you work out too hard, you not only risk injury, but you also lose the healing benefits of exercise. I disagree with the "No Pain, No Gain" philosophy. I say if it hurts, stop immediately. Listen to your body.

LOVE YOURSELF BY DRINKING PURE WATER

You've seen the stories for years in major magazines and newspapers around the country: Tap water is full of deadly chemicals. Don't drink tap water. Buy distilled, or purified water or a reverse osmosis system. Most people don't drink enough water. If you make a habit of drinking eight glasses of water a day, you won't be tempted to drink a lot of soda pop or coffee. Invest in your health. Buy pure water and drink plenty of it.

ELIMINATION

Proper elimination is extremely important to your health. Take the time to use the bathroom often. It is important to go to the toilet immediately when you feel the urge. The colon moves the toxic waste out of the body with muscle contractions known as peristaltic waves. These waves only last a few minutes. If you think, "I'll wait until later," when "later" comes, you'll sit on the toilet and nothing will happen. The waves have stopped. The time has passed. The habit of "waiting until later" is a major cause of health problems.

From kindergarten on we are trained to ignore our own physical messages about going to the bathroom in order to fit someone else's schedule. Many fully grown adults still think they are supposed to wait until "the proper time."

A man told me, "I know I should drink more water but I can't. My boss will fire me if I go to the bathroom that much." This fear is usually unfounded. A supervisor may disapprove if excessive time is spent in the bathroom but I doubt that anyone would be fired for that reason.

I was in a business meeting years ago. In the middle of the boss's talk Tom got up and said, "I'm going to the bathroom."

The boss said, "This will only take a few more minutes."

Tom said with a smile, "When you've got to go, you've got to go," and walked off.

Everyone laughed—including the boss.

Kathy, a psychologist, said, "It's been such a relief to know it's O.K. to go to the bathroom whenever I need to. I thought it would be unprofessional to interrupt my work. Now I just say, 'Would you excuse me? I'll be back in a few minutes'."

Constipation is a serious health hazard. It is better to use a laxative than to suffer. Health food stores are a good place to find natural supplements that aid the body in eliminating waste.

LOVE YOUR BODY BY RESTING

At one time I had a problem with severe headaches. About once a week I'd get a pain in my head so bad that I had to lie down and rest. That's all I could do. One night as I was lying there, angry that I was unable to work, I thought to myself, "You know, if I'm going to take a night off like this every week, I ought to do something fun."

I heard a voice say, "We thought you'd never get it." I decided to schedule a day off every week and just relax and rest. When I did so, I no longer experienced headaches.

Some people need more rest than others. Listen to your own body and rest when you are tired. I asked Jill, "What changes have you made since you've been listening to your body?" She said, "I rest when I'm tired and I exercise when I have energy."

Mark said, "I've been going to bed earlier and the pain in my back is gone. I was tired. I was just plain tired."

ACKNOWLEDGE YOURSELF FOR IMPROVING

It takes effort to develop good health care habits. Rather than trying to change everything at once, praise yourself for every little improvement you make. Tell yourself, "I love my body," every time you say no to dessert. Think, "I love myself," every time you stop what you are doing and take a drink of water. When you feel tired and you take the time to rest, acknowledge, "I'm listening to my body."

Little changes make a big difference. If you don't have time to walk for twenty minutes, take a five minute walk. Do what you can and feel good about it. Rather than criticizing yourself for all the things you didn't do, acknowledge yourself for all the many ways that you do listen to your body.

LISTEN TO YOUR DREAMS

In biblical times, God frequently spoke to people in their dreams. He still does. You can receive answers directly from God in your sleep. The first step is to write down exactly what you want to know. For example, "Dear God, what is causing this pain?" or "I want to know what I need to do to heal _____." Tell yourself before you go to bed, "I will remember my dreams tonight."

Keep a pen and a pad of paper by your bed and write down your dreams as soon as you wake up. Even if you only remember a fragment of a dream, write it down. As you begin writing you will probably remember more details. Write down how you felt during the dream as well as what was happening.

If you don't get a clear answer the first night, repeat the same procedure the next evening. Usually within three nights you'll receive your message. At the end of three days, read everything you wrote down. The answer is there.

I wrote down, "What do I need to do to increase my energy?" In my dream I heard a voice. It said, "Stay away from sugar." I didn't like this message. For a few days I argued, "I don't eat that much sugar." But finally I told myself, "I asked the question and got an answer. I'll never know if it's correct unless I try it." I got up every morning and prayed, "Dear God, help me to stay away from sugar today." I still wanted sugary foods but I was able to resist. I had been much more addicted to sugar than I had realized. Soon I was guided to take a supplement (chromium picolinate) that eliminated the cravings completely.

I once wrote this question before going to bed: "Dear God, what is it I most need to know?"

That night God appeared to me in a dream as a man with the most loving eyes I've ever seen. He said, "You still don't get that you've never done anything that offended me."

CHAPTER 6

Forgiveness: The Heart of Healing

FORGIVENESS IS ALWAYS HEALING

I felt a large swollen knot on the inside of Joan's left ankle. I massaged it a while. Joan, a woman in her forties, said, "That's been swollen since I was a kid. I was hit with a rock when I was eleven and it's never healed."

I said, "You need to forgive whoever threw that rock."

She laughed, "You got that right. It was my brother, and I'm still mad at him."

I told her to write this forgiveness affirmation ten times every day for a week. "I, Joan, completely forgive Bobby for hurting me." When I saw her a week later her ankle was completely normal.

RESENTMENT INTERFERES WITH HEALING

Condemnation of yourself and others hurts your body. It takes a lot of energy to hold a grudge. Carrying around hate, anger and guilt is like carrying a fifty-pound sack on your back. It is difficult to reach a higher state of health, happiness or prosperity when you're lugging around heavy emotional baggage from the past.

Forgiveness is the bottom line of healing. There can be no permanent progress without it. Forgiveness is another word for healing. The quicker you forgive, the faster you will heal.

In her book, *Loving Relationships*, Sondra Ray calls forgiveness emotional disarmament. "It is giving up all desire for revenge or getting even." Forgiveness is a way of putting the past behind you where it belongs. Forgiveness frees you from the past so that you can be happy now. The past has no power to affect you now, unless you choose to think so.

If you find it difficult to forgive yourself or others, think of it as *seeing what happened differently*. Forgiveness is not pardoning a guilt. It is a willingness to see that no one is guilty, including you. Forgiveness is changing your thinking about what happened. It happens quickly when you are willing to reinterpret the situation with compassion for everyone involved, including yourself. Forgiveness is the willingness to accept a new interpretation that brings you peace.

There is no sin. The word sin is an archery term that means to miss the mark. It does not mean an offense that must be punished. It's just a mistake. There is no mistake that can not be corrected by God; therefore, there can be no sin. It is our own arrogance that tells us that some mistakes are unforgivable. We think of God as unforgiving because we are so unwilling to forgive.

GOD IS GRACE

Like a loving mother who always loves her children no matter what they do, God always loves you unconditionally. God is merciful because God is Love. The grace of God is much more than forgiveness. It is a firm promise that you are always loved no matter what.

God's grace is a constant blessing that is always manifesting every detail of your life for your highest good and happiness. Grace means that at any moment you can realize the truth of your divine birthright as a holy child of God. In an instant you can know your divine innocence and receive your inheritance of peace, love, joy and abundant blessings.

GOD ONLY BLESSES

Do you think of God as a judgmental old man who sits in heaven keeping count of every mistake you have ever made so that he can punish you? That was my picture of God before I had an actual experience of God's presence. When I found The Great Spirit for myself I found nothing but love. I also found that it is my own judgment that condemns me, not God. It is the sentence I pass on myself and others that causes me pain.

Because we are all connected, whatever I think or do regarding other people, I also think and do to myself. I reap the natural consequences of my thoughts and actions, be they good or not so good. If I send love to others I will surely receive love back from others. It may not be from the same people but, in the flow of life, I get back what I give.

If I think hateful thoughts or do unkind deeds, then I am giving a negative energy to life. This energy will come back to me like a boomerang: not to punish me, but to show me a reflection of that part of myself. Your world is like a mirror. Life reflects back to you the energy you put into it.

Before I discovered this truth, driving was a horrible experience for me. Every day people would honk their horns at me, yell obscenities and make vulgar gestures. From behind the wheel, the world seemed a terrible, loveless place.

After I started sending God's Love, I began to notice how unforgiving and impatient I was in the car. If a bus stopped in front of me to unload passengers, I felt personally offended. When people cut me off, I thought they were mean and nasty—deliberately going out of their way to annoy me.

After some time I began to notice that I also cut people off. I didn't intend to be unkind. I just made mistakes. Sometimes I forgot to look. Other times my judgment was off. I made a pledge to myself never to honk my own car horn in anger, to bless people who cut me off and to send love to the other drivers no matter what. As I did this, driving became a completely different experience. I still live in the same big city. There's still heavy traffic every day, but it has been many years since anyone has waved me a finger or honked at me in anger. It just doesn't happen to me because I'm not putting out that kind of negative energy any more.

What most people do when they want to improve their life is to try to change what's "out there." We look for healing out there. We think the problems and the solutions are out there. So we are always looking outside ourselves for the answers. We will be disappointed unless we look within our own mind to understand that our attitude is the problem. There's nothing out there but God holding up a mirror.

A man was diagnosed as having terminal cancer. His doctors told him he would die within a year. He took his savings and went to a tropical island resort for a vacation. There he met a monk who told him, "Cancer is within your mind. If you want to heal the cancer, heal your mind first, and the cancer will disappear." The monk taught this man how to meditate on God. The man went back home and meditated on the presence of God every day. A few months later his doctors were surprised to find that the cancer was completely gone.

Contemplating the presence of God is healing because when you have a direct experience of God, you know the source of all life, love and healing. When you have direct communication with God, you know that God is grace.

FORGIVE YOURSELF

God has absolutely no desire to punish you for anything you did in the past. God never condemns you in the first place. The only condemnation that exists is self-condemnation.

Your only responsibility is to accept forgiveness for yourself. Allow God to heal the false idea of guilt in your mind. Guilt is not real. Whenever you think anyone is guilty you are mistaken. No one is guilty. Nothing that happens is anyone's fault. Giving up the belief in guilt is the key to healing. Accepting forgiveness for yourself is the heart of healing.

In any situation where you feel angry or resentful you can be sure that you also feel guilty. In fact everything that you think you dislike about others is an attempt to project your own guilt (which isn't real) onto the other person.

Whenever you think another person is guilty you must also believe that you are also guilty. After all, you were involved too. Behind every attempt to blame someone else is the idea, "If only I had done something differently."

Think about someone you dislike or a situation that is upsetting to you. Do this now. Ask yourself, Why do I feel guilty? What is it I think I did wrong?

Healing always involves letting go of the guilt within your own mind. Most folks find it much easier to forgive others than to forgive themselves. This unwillingness to forgive oneself is actually insanity. It is the crazy notion that suffering helps.

Deloris, who was at least a hundred pounds overweight, shared, "Twenty years ago I had a four year old daughter. I had to have surgery so I asked my mother to take care of my daughter while I was recovering. My mother said, 'I don't want to even see that half breed!' When I came home from the hospital I was groggy from the anesthesia and I slept for a long time. When I woke up I found my daughter's dead body in the pool. She had drowned while I was sleeping."

Would you forgive Deloris? Even if she had deliberately murdered her child, by law she would be forgiven after twenty years. But could you forgive yourself if you were her? Who does it help for Deloris to feel guilty?

I ask all my students to make a list of the people they need to forgive, including all the situations they need to forgive themselves for. Then I say, "Start by forgiving yourself."

There is no need to feel guilty about anything you did in the past. The truth is, you were doing the best you could at the time. All human beings make mistakes. If we didn't make mistakes we would not learn what works and what doesn't. Parents want their children to avoid mistakes, yet children are here to learn and their mistakes are their best teachers.

Larry said, "If I forgive myself when I make a mistake, won't that allow me to do it again?"

I said, "Feeling guilty will not make me change my behavior. Forgiveness will help me to change. If I feel guilty about something I've done, then I'm likely to repeat the mistake. For example, if I eat half a chocolate pie, and I punish myself by feeling guilty, then I will probably eat the other half. But if I forgive myself then I can simply acknowledge I made a mistake and go on with life in a positive direction."

Feeling guilty never does any good at all.

The feeling of guilt is a form of self-punishment. When we feel guilty, we will punish ourselves before anyone else gets the chance. Much pain is self-inflicted punishment resulting from the feeling of guilt.

You don't deserve to be punished, regardless of what you've done in the past. God doesn't want you to suffer. If you did something that seemed to cause harm, God wants to heal you, not punish you. God wants to correct the mistake. Love's only desire is to love.

God will save you from the consequences of your mistakes if you ask God to help you forgive yourself. God will heal and correct your thinking. God will help you to accept the truth of your eternal innocence. Ask for His help.

Self-condemnation and guilt create a feeling of unworthiness. God withholds nothing from you. She gladly gives you health, love, prosperity and every good thing you ask for. But if you feel unworthy of the good things in life, then you will unconsciously refuse to accept them, even when the good stuff is given to you giftwrapped and free of charge. You'll do something to ensure failure when things are going too well for your guilty conscience.

You deserve to be healthy and happy no matter what you have done in the past. You deserve peace, success and love. The feeling of guilt or unworthiness is a sure sign that forgiveness is needed. You can grant yourself a pardon. You can forgive yourself.

The way that people usually go about forgiving themselves is to think a vague idea about forgiveness once in a while. It is a haphazard approach that is rarely successful.

There is a way to forgive yourself that really works. It is writing forgiveness affirmations. Writing forgiveness affirmations is a systematic program that never fails. When you write a specific forgiveness affirmation ten times a day for one week, you impress your subconscious mind with your willingness to forgive. Your thinking changes and your emotions change as well.

Personally, I have found it effective to write a forgiveness affirmation ten times a day for one week. Jesus was asked how many times we should forgive our brother. He said seventy times seven. If you write a forgiveness affirmation seventy times a day for seven days, even the guilt that seemed "super-glued" to you before will dissolve away forever.

ASK GOD FOR HELP

When you sit down to write your forgiveness affirmations, take a moment to say a prayer. Ask God to help you forgive.

God will gladly remove all bad feelings if you ask Him to do so. But if you don't ask, then God will not interfere with your free will.

Pray, "Dear God, I am willing to forgive myself. Please correct my thinking and remove all feeling of guilt. Thank you."

Some affirmations for self-forgiveness are:

God is helping me to forgive myself now.
God has already forgiven me. I completely forgive myself now.
I completely forgive myself for
I, {your name}, am an innocent child of God.

Choose one affirmation. Read it out loud. Then write it ten to seventy times. Each time you write it, speak the words aloud. Writing and speaking the forgiveness affirmation helps you by involving your senses of hearing, seeing and feeling. It is always healing to hear yourself speak words of forgiveness.

FORGIVE OTHERS

In her book *Songs of the Night*, Gian Michael Salvato tells how she completely healed herself of AIDS. She got the virus as a result of being raped by two men, but one of the healing principles she adopted was, "I release the need for blame or guilt." She said, "It's no one's fault that I have AIDS," and the virus disappeared.

Forgiving others will always be healing to you. Anytime you hold a grudge toward another human being, it affects your own life in a negative way. If you want forgiveness, you can only feel worthy of it by giving it to others. It is necessary to forgive others in order to completely accept forgiveness for yourself.

By forgiving yourself, you acknowledge your own humanity: "I made a mistake." Other people are human beings who make mistakes, too. Everyone makes mistakes but they still deserve your forgiveness.

If you think another person is undeserving of health and happiness, you will withhold it from yourself as well. This is so because the subconscious part of your mind cannot believe something is true for others but not for you. Whatever you believe about others you *must* also believe about yourself. If you think anyone deserves to suffer, you will also believe that you deserve to suffer and you will create misery for yourself.

For example, Tim is a vegetarian who had cancer. We explored his beliefs about who deserves punishment. Tim strongly believed people who eat meat deserve to get cancer and die because of their cruelty to animals. He changed his belief by writing this forgiveness affirmation. I, Tim, completely forgive everyone who eats meat. He recovered his health quickly.

You need to forgive anyone you think has hurt you in any way. You need to do this for your own sake, not theirs. They may be gone from this earth, but you can still forgive them because forgiveness happens inside your mind.

Forgiveness means that you simply let go of the feelings that are hurting you. You release all hurt, bitterness, anger and criticism. Forgiving others does not mean you have to *do* anything. It just means that you let go of the negative emotions you hold about others. Such forgiveness does not mean that you agree with what they did. You don't have to like their behavior. You don't have to go see them, kiss and make up or even speak to them.

Sherry, a woman in her forties, asked, "Do you have to confront the person you're forgiving?"

I said, "No! Forgiveness happens within your mind. In some cases it may be good to talk to the person, but it is certainly not necessary."

She volunteered, "I was sexually abused as a child. I can't seem to forgive the person who abused me. My therapist says I'll have to confront him before I can get over this."

I said, "That is a major misconception about forgiveness. We think the other person has to do something: admit they were wrong, apologize or make amends of some sort. Or we think they should be grateful for our forgiveness. NO! We forgive for our own peace of mind. You don't even have to speak to the other person. All you need to do is be willing to forgive."

When people say, "I can't forgive _____," I say, "The truth is you are *unwilling* to forgive."

With the tiniest willingness on your part, God will remove all the feelings of hatred, anger and bitterness. The emotional wounds of the past can be forgiven and healed now.

YOU CAN SEE THE PAST DIFFERENTLY

God will help you to forgive by giving you a new perspective on what happened. God will help you to see the past in a new light. You will be given an interpretation of the past that brings you peace of mind. The truth is no one can really hurt you. Only your interpretation of what others did can hurt you. It's never *what happened* that's the problem. It's what you decided it *meant*. The problem is you stopped giving love.

People come to me for counseling and they tell me, "My parents abused me. My husband beat me. My girlfriend left me." And so on. Then they announce, "And that's why I'm miserable!"

I say, "BALONEY! You can not be unhappy about *what happened* in the past. You can only be upset by *your interpretation* of what happened. You decided it meant something unloving about yourself. 'My parents abused me, therefore they didn't love me.' 'My ex-husband beat me, therefore there's something wrong with me.' 'My girlfriend left me, therefore I'll never have a good relationship'."

Dottie shared, "My mother beat me with a belt when I was five. The physical pain was soon gone, but my interpretation of what that meant hurt me for twenty years. I concluded from what happened that she didn't love me, and so I wasn't going to love her, either. My interpretation was wrong."

This simple test tells you when your perceptions of the past are untrue: if you are not at peace about what happened, your perception is false.

Rebecca, who was sexually abused as a girl, said, "For years I was a professional victim. Then my spiritual teacher said, 'This victim stuff is a drag. You've got to come up with an empowering interpretation of what happened'." Rebecca prayed and asked God to help her see the truth. She was given a different explanation for why she experienced abuse. "I came to this earth to be a powerful woman. I didn't want to abuse that power, so I chose a family

FORGIVENESS: THE HEART OF HEALING

situation where I could learn what it felt like when people abused power." She is indeed a powerful and kind woman today.

Here is my interpretation. My soul's mission on earth is to learn to forgive. I chose a family situation and some relationships that would give me opportunities to learn what forgiveness is.

When you reinterpret the past with God's Love you will still remember what happened, but the memories will not be painful. The emotional charge will be gone. You will be grateful for the wisdom you gained from those experiences—deeply grateful.

If you hold on to a grievance, what you are doing is withholding love from yourself. You obstruct the flow of life in your body when you carry a grudge. Love has to flow through you if you are to stay healthy. If you are physically sick or overweight, that is a good indication that you have forgiveness work to do. If you are anything but peaceful, you have need of forgiveness.

YOU CAN CHOOSE PEACE

In group discussions about forgiveness, it is easy to see that resentment is a state of mind which is *chosen*. It really doesn't have anything to do with what happened. One person is resentful because she was sexually assaulted. Another person is even more upset because his parents promised him a pony and didn't deliver.

It is human nature to think that when others do things to us we don't like, it is unforgivable. We think we have a right to be resentful because what happened was so terrible. That's what we tell ourselves—but it's not true.

Failure to forgive anyone hurts you. It doesn't matter whether it's a little offense or a huge one in your mind. There is no difference between holding a small grudge or a major one. Any grievance that is unforgiven will hurt your peace of mind, and peace of mind is the foundation of health.

With tears in her eyes, a woman told how shocked and upset she felt when her son got married several years ago and didn't invite her to the wedding. After a long discussion I said, "These kinds of hurts are just part of the human experience. Everyone goes through their share. That's not important. The hard knocks and heartaches of life only hurt for as long as we hang on to the unloving thoughts. As soon as we are willing to accept another interpretation, or see what happened from a loving perspective, we are at peace. We don't have to suffer for years. We can forgive, and let go. Can you think of a good reason why a person might get married without inviting his mother?"

She thought for a moment and said, "Maybe it was just easier for them to have a small wedding. Maybe they were overwhelmed with their own feelings and didn't know it would be important to me."

The painful thought that causes resentment is, "They were trying to hurt me." This is the line of thinking beneath a great deal of anger. Regardless of how much someone else may have hurt you in the past, they weren't trying to hurt you. If you were abused it was because the abuser was terrified. They were insane with fear. They were sick.

If you look at the past of any abuser, you will always find trauma. As you become willing to forgive, you begin to understand that this person was in terrible pain. They were doing the best they could at the time with the background and knowledge they had.

Human beings are very stingy with forgiveness. We tend to wait until our own pain is intense before we are willing to forgive others. We bang our head against a brick wall over and over until we are finally ready for a change of heart. We prefer to blame others for our problem rather than realize that it is our own unloving thinking that is causing the pain.

FORGIVE YOUR PARENTS

Three people extremely important to forgive: yourself, your father and your mother.

Your relationship with your parents is a powerful mold from which all other relationships take form. Regardless of whether your mother and father are still living on this earth, you have a relationship with them in your mind. The quality of this relationship, whether it is loving or bitter, determines the quality of your life.

Your feelings about your parents do affect your health. Resentment or bitter feelings toward anyone can cause physical problems, but unhappy feelings about your parents are especially important to heal.

The reason it is so important to forgive your mother and father is this. Your subconscious mind associates all women with your mother and all men with your father. Whatever you really feel about your mother deep down inside, you will transfer to every other female, including yourself if you are a woman. The feeling you have toward your father, you will project onto every other male, including yourself if you are a man.

If you resent your mother you will tend to have difficulty in relationships with women. Likewise your relationships with men will tend to be problem-ridden if you resent your father.

FORGIVENESS MAKES MEMORIES SWEET

Resentment is a cover for love. If you feel intense hatred or anger toward another, you can be certain that you love them deeply. If you didn't love them, you wouldn't care. You would be indifferent. You only bother to hold a grudge against those from whom you want love and approval—the people whom, in fact, you love. Intense feelings are a testimony of love. Forgiveness uncovers the love that was there all along.

Once when I was visiting my mother, we got into a loud argument over something that happened when I was six years old. I took a walk to a nearby park. As I sat down on a bench I prayed for help.

Immediately I heard a voice saying, "If you didn't love her, you wouldn't care."

It's never too late to have a happy childhood. Because the past exists in your mind, you can change your past by changing your mind about what happened. I used to say my childhood was a nightmare of one trauma after another. But as I forgave my parents, my siblings and myself, I began to remember the many loving times we shared. Now the memories of my family's kindness and caring are more important and plentiful than memories of the occasions when I felt hurt or neglected.

One little resentment can make our entire past seem bitter. Forgiveness makes memories sweet. When we feel angry we will find in our memories exactly what we are looking for: reasons to be upset. But when we forgive, love is what we remember.

Here are some forgiveness affirmations to help you forgive your parents:

"God is helping me to forgive my mother now."
"God is helping me to forgive my father now."
"I completely forgive my mother for   ."
"I now forgive my father for   ."
"My mother is innocent and I am innocent."
"My father is innocent and I am innocent."

EXERCISE YOUR FORGIVENESS MUSCLES

Forgiveness is a continuing process. Like cleaning your house, it has to be done on a regular basis. The more you forgive yourself and others, the healthier, happier and more successful you become. Sometimes I think I've forgiven someone, but when I least expect it, anger will flare up about something that is past and gone. Then I know I've got more forgiveness to do. I need to forgive myself for my involvement in the situation and I need to forgive everyone else involved.

Practice forgiveness every day of your life. Forgive the guy who parked in your space this morning. Forgive yourself for interpreting his actions as unloving. Forgive your lunch date who was ten minutes late. And forgive yourself when you make mistakes.

The following affirmation is a good one to write, think, and speak every day. "I forgive everyone and everything that may need forgiveness, including myself."

Be generous with forgiveness and you will become aware of the grace of God that is generously given to you.

God will help you forgive the people you can't seem to forgive by yourself. Just pray, "God, I am willing to forgive _____. Please help me."

Make a list of everyone you feel any resentment or anger toward. Include everyone you dislike. Write down the name of everyone who you think:
Hurt you.
Cheated you.
Left you.
Lied to you.
Didn't support you.
Owes you something.
Deserves punishment.

Make your list now. Writing down the names will help you to heal yourself. Sam, who was suffering with severe arthritis, insisted that he did not resent or feel anger toward anyone. But when he came to the question, "Who owes you something?" he said, "I think a lot of people owe me."

Thinking that someone owes you something is a form of resentment. No one owes you anything. How can you be free when you hold others in bondage in your mind?

Choose one person you are willing to forgive and write your own forgiveness affirmation. "God is helping me to forgive _____ for _____."

Write this affirmation ten to seventy times every day for seven days. A week from now you will feel much better—and freer.

LET IT GO

A Native American forgiveness ritual is to write down the experience that seemed to cause you pain, or make a symbol for it. Then you burn or bury the paper or symbol. As you ignite it or cover it with dirt, you vow never to speak of it again.

After writing your forgiveness affirmations for a week, bury the papers in the ground or burn them. Vow to yourself not to mention it again.

If you truly don't feel ready to let it go forever, you may need to write more forgiveness affirmations. Or you may need to see a therapist. It is important that you don't try to rush the healing process too fast. However, most of the guilt and anger we suffer from is just ancient garbage that must be released sooner or later. We tend to get attached to the interpretations or stories of our past. These stories become a part of our identity. We hang on to them for the wrong reasons. We want to be right, or we use the past as an excuse for not choosing happiness now.

You have the power to change your thinking. You do choose which thoughts you dwell on and which you release. When a thought of guilt (your own or someone else's) comes to mind, you can choose to see it differently or dismiss it entirely. It's not the occasional random thoughts that matter. It's the ones you entertain over and over that make your life and health what it is.

Choose thoughts that bring you peace, and health will surely increase.

FORGIVENESS BRINGS BLESSING

James had been trying, without success, for over a year to find financing to expand his business. When he did the six week healing program, he did an excellent job of forgiving everyone. He thought back to his earliest memories and made a list of everyone he needed to forgive. Every day for a week he wrote and spoke, "I, James, am willing to forgive everyone and everything including myself."

On the day after he burned his list a wealthy acquaintance phoned him and said, "I have a million dollars I want to invest in your business."

Is it worth your time to practice forgiveness? To James it was worth a million dollars.

CHAPTER 7

Letting Go

MAKE ROOM FOR MIRACLES

You have to clear out the old to make room for new blessings. To create a better life quickly, let go of the people and things you no longer want. If your life is cluttered up with relationships, possessions and activities you no longer delight in, then there is no space for something better to enter your life.

I learned about the healing power of letting go by reading Catherine Ponder's books. She calls it "forming a vacuum." She says nature abhors a vacuum, so whenever you get rid of worn-out things and worn-out relationships, something new and better will rush in to fill the space.

LET PEOPLE GO

Do you spend your time with people you don't enjoy, respect or admire? It is common for people to hold on to relationships that are clearly unhealthy. What is an unhealthy relationship? Any association that drains you of energy is unhealthy. If you feel that someone drags you down more often than they lift you up, that relationship is unhealthy.

Physical abuse is obviously unhealthy. However, for some individuals this fact can be difficult to see for these reasons. They grew up around violent behavior. They refuse to face reality. They continue to hope the violent person will change.

I have a woman friend who had a female roommate. One day her roommate punched her. The violent blow damaged my friend's back. I suggested she evict the violent woman, but she really wanted the living arrangement to work out. These two women had been friends for more than twenty-five years. I said, "If someone is violent, they will not change to suit you. She is likely to assault you again."

My friend would not face the reality that her roommate had become violent. Her body paid the price less than a month later. Her roommate beat her up again. This time she got a court order and forced her to move.

Verbal abuse can be just as unhealthy as physical abuse. If you allow people to say unkind, untrue or demeaning things to you, they will continue to do so. Those with low self-esteem may keep "friends" who verbally abuse them terribly. A man came to me for a healing treatment. I asked him what he wanted to heal. He said, "I want to heal my shame."

I said a prayer and asked God to heal the feelings of shame. He told me later that he became aware that the woman he shared a house with was trying to use shame to manipulate him. Now he didn't allow her to do so. He would just say, "That's not true." It wasn't long before he moved out and left that unhealthy relationship.

Dishonesty is a sign of an unhealthy relationship. Honesty is a basic requirement for a good association of any kind. If truthful communication is not present, if someone says one thing and does another or omits important information, it may be wise to release them to their divine good elsewhere.

If you know from past experience that a certain person does not keep his or her agreements, or that he or she doesn't tell the whole truth, don't expect them to change. People do change, of course, but they won't change for you. They change only when they are ready to do so for their own reasons.

Why bother with dishonest people? There are plenty of others who value integrity. Care enough for yourself to recognize the sacredness of honest, supportive relationships. Spend your time with people you admire rather than in destructive situations.

Neglect is another indication of an unhealthy relationship. If you are doing all the giving while receiving little or nothing back, you are allowing yourself to be neglected. If I notice that it's me who calls and offers invitations without reciprocation, I stop calling. A relationship requires the participation of both parties. You are responsible for keeping the giving and receiving balanced.

When selecting friends, look for people who keep their word. Look for people who share themselves generously with you, people with whom you can speak openly, heart to heart. Choose givers. Release the takers. If a relationship is more work than fun, it's unhealthy.

BOUNDARIES ARE HEALTHY

When people hear about the healing power of love and forgiveness, they sometimes misinterpret these divine healing powers to mean unconditional tolerance of any behavior. It is a mistake to think that we should love and forgive everyone no matter what they do *and still associate with them.* Forgiveness may be our spiritual duty, but hanging on to others is not.

Unconditional love does not mean unconditional involvement. It is insane to continue to do business with or socialize with people who are not good for you. Physical and verbal abuse, dishonesty and neglect are not God's will for you.

Love and forgiveness have to do with your inner experience, how you think and feel inside. This does not necessarily mean spending time with a particular individual or group. In fact, associating with the wrong people can hinder your spiritual growth and healing just as much as resentment does. It is possible to throw someone out of your house without throwing them out of your heart. Forgiveness means wishing them well.

Boundaries are where you draw the line regarding what kind of behavior you will and will not tolerate from others. It is important to be clear within your own mind as to what kind of behavior you will not put up with. When your boundaries are clear, no one will step over your line. People intuitively know what your limits are.

One way to set your boundaries is to draw a large circle on a piece of paper. Inside the circle write down all the things that give you joy. Write down the kinds of experiences you are willing to have. Now make the symbolic boundary of the circle thicker. This is called a medicine shield in Native American tribes.

Outside the circle write down the kinds of experiences you are unwilling to have. Include the experiences you will become involved in by invitation only, for example, a visit from a long, lost relative.

The first time I drew a medicine shield, I was receiving six to ten phone calls a day from people trying to sell me things I didn't want. On the outside of the circle I wrote NO SALES CALLS. Not a single sales person phoned me for months.

Having written boundaries helps you remember to say no to unhealthy situations. You can choose not to participate with:

People who are abusing alcohol or drugs.
Conversations that are inappropriately critical or sexual.

Unasked-for advice.
People wanting a handout.

Make your own list. Write down your boundaries. Set your limits. Children will try all kinds of behavior to discover where your boundaries are drawn. They need to know your limits. Adults do the same thing in both business and personal relationships.

You tend to get from others whatever you are willing to put up with. When your boundaries are firm in your own mind, others intuitively know what you will not tolerate and they will not try to push you. People will notice what you allow and what you don't. If you don't communicate when unacceptable behavior is occurring, they will keep on doing it. Writing down your boundaries is a way of defining for yourself the terms of your relationships.

For example, Greg told me that he used to get angry and frustrated with his mother. Whenever they went to a movie together she would always start talking during the show. Her jabbering disturbed him, and the people around them as well. But Greg felt it would be disrespectful to tell his mother how he felt. After defining his boundaries, however, he did tell her he would not go to the movies with her if she was going to talk during the film. She changed her behavior and they now enjoy going to the movies together.

Clear boundaries make it easier for you to separate how you feel from the behavior of others. It is a way of affirming that you can choose to feel peaceful regardless of what others do. Let others live their lives the way they choose, without affecting your choice.

"I'M WILLING TO LET GO"

The willingness to release people is a healthy attitude of detachment. In order to relate to others in a healthy way, you must be willing to let them go. In many cases just the willingness alone will restore harmony.

Jim said, "I have a lot of friends and I'm grateful for them. However, I realized this week I was spending too much time with them. I was exhausted from so many phone calls from them. I didn't have any time to just relax and unwind. This week they gave me more space and I didn't even say anything. I just emotionally released them."

When you are emotionally willing to let others go it becomes much easier to communicate openly and resolve problems. Relationships become deeper and closer through honest communication. If, through fear of losing a friend or loved one, you don't talk about issues that disturb you, the unspoken emotions will inevitably destroy the relationship. Rapport dies without authentic sharing of thoughts and feelings. When you release your attachment to a certain outcome, you will be able to iron out most relationship problems through communication.

However, at times the divine plan calls for parting company. If that is the case, it will happen in a way that is peaceful. Whether you are physically together or not, your willingness to release people and let them go helps maintain harmony in the relationship.

A relationship is not over when you physically go your separate ways. Relationships are eternal because love is eternal. We are all one life forever whether our bodies are together or not. You will always love everyone that you have ever loved. You have no choice about that. You do choose whether or not to be with a certain person.

The attitude with which you depart is very important. If you leave with blame or bitterness, you will hurt yourself. The unloving thoughts cause you, not them, pain. When you release people, let them go with God's Love and a blessing.

MAKE A GRACEFUL EXIT

People change and grow in different directions. You may need to be the one to say "Adios." It's time to move on. For example, if you become involved in spiritual activities that your friend disapproves of, you no longer value the same things. The two of you are not interested in the same subjects anymore. You'll know when it's best to wave good-bye.

Bless yourself when you move on. God has many wonderful ways of bringing you companionship. Don't limit your good by trying to get all of your warm fuzzies from one specific person or group. The truth is you don't need anyone to give you love. Love comes from God. All you need do to receive God's Love is to inhale.

TRUST GOD

Prepare for surprises when you write and speak the words of release this week. Some of the people who will leave your life may be ones you wanted to keep around. The first time I spoke the releasing affirmation, *"I now release everyone and everything that is no longer for my highest good,"* three friends who I was seeing on a weekly basis phoned to say, "I don't really want to do this anymore." If I had not been consciously releasing, I might have been upset by these changes. Instead, I just thought, "God is making a space for new people to come into my life for my greater good."

Welcome changes with open arms. Trust God to provide everything you need, and you will soon discover that healthy, loving relationships, fulfilling activities, prosperity, joy and exuberant health are yours.

Bless the people who release you. Let go and trust God. Whatever leaves your physical presence, let it go. Bless the people who move on and bless yourself for leaving.

GOD WILL DO THE PRUNING

Every gardener knows the importance of pruning plants. If I don't cut back my rose bushes, they stop blooming. When my citrus trees become overgrown, the quality of the fruit is sacrificed. Releasing unsatisfying situations is just as important as thinning out a garden. Yet you don't have to do anything except be willing to let go.

When I talk about the healing power of letting go, I often hear comments like: "I don't like my job but I can't quit. I'm not happy in my marriage but I can't leave." I'm not saying to quit your job or divorce your spouse. If you are willing to let God remove whatever is not for your best interest, it will happen easily and peacefully. You don't have to personally decide what to do. Just be willing to let go.

A nurse named Debbie shared that she was not getting along with her boss. The situation bothered her very much. During the discussion about releasing people, I told her, "If you are willing to release your boss this week you will either get a new boss or a new job. If that doesn't happen then it's not divine order and it means you are supposed to learn to get along with her."

Two weeks later she announced that her boss had quit and now she was the supervisor. "I never thought this would happen, but while I was writing, *I am willing to release everything and everyone that is no longer for my highest good,* things were going on that I didn't know about. My company decided to eliminate one position, my job. They offered my ex-boss more hours and a pay raise but she turned it down. Now I'm in charge, working full time instead of part time."

LET GO OF THINGS

The Bible says, "There is a time for everything, and a season for every activity under heaven.... a time to search and a time to give up, a time to keep and a time to throw away." (Ecclesiastes 3:1,6)

Most people are better at keeping than they are at throwing away. Releasing physical things is symbolic of letting go of the past. It prepares space for your new life to materialize and it puts unused items into circulation. When you look at something in your environment that you no longer want or use, it drains your energy. You have to walk around it, dust it or shuffle through it in order to find what you really want.

Juliet said, "I had cancer, high blood pressure, a hiatal hernia and ringing in my ears. I felt terrible and I was spending a fortune on medicine. I had a drawer full of pills that I had to take every day and I was getting worse. Six months ago I read an article in the paper that said it's good to get rid of things you no longer use. My house was crowded with antiques and collections that I was tired of dusting, so I had a garage sale and sold them all. An old friend came to the garage sale and brought me a bottle of some liquid dietary supplement. I started taking it and I began to feel better right away. Now I have no cancer, my blood pressure is normal, the ringing in my ears is gone and there's no hiatal hernia. I only take two pills a day. I feel wonderful and I'm making an extra five hundred dollars a month distributing this product."

When I heard Juliet tell her story, I recognized right away that she had used the healing power of letting go. She released the things in her house that she no longer used. This letting go of the old made way for her new good to come to her. The health product was exactly what she needed. It came to her because she created a space for something fresh.

I tell my students, "Go through the entire house and throw out, sell, or give away everything that you no longer want. Release everything that doesn't inspire you. Get rid of all those books you don't read, the records you don't listen to, the dishes you never use, and even the old underwear in the back of your drawer that you've been saving in case of a laundry crisis."

If you haven't used it in a year, let it go. You probably won't use it next year, if you didn't need it last year.

Be sure to get rid of all the food in your kitchen that you don't really want to eat. This is especially important if you want to release body weight. Clean out your refrigerator, freezer and cupboards.

Tamara, a divorced woman, had not been in a romantic relationship for six years. As she was cleaning out her storage room, she found her old wedding dress. She gave it to a charity, and immediately afterwards met a wonderful man and fell in love. She was so excited she called her divorced sister and said, "Dump the dress."

Michelle, whose son died several years ago at age twenty, told me, "I finally gave away my son's coat last week."

"That's wonderful!" I said.

"I held on to it all this time, because it smelled like him."

I said, "You've really released him to God now. It's great, too, because someone who needed a coat is getting some good out of it. Releasing things always opens up a space for your divine good to come to you." Soon after that, she accepted an opportunity to move to a foreign country. Her letters tell me she's never been happier.

LET "YOUR" DISEASE GO

If you want to let a malady go, be sure that you don't call it *yours*. People say, "my arthritis . . .," "my cancer," "my pain." I say, "Don't call it *yours* if you want to release it." *My* is possessive. Don't use it unless you want to possess the illness.

"How can I speak of it, then?" a woman asked.

You can say, "the disease" if you must speak of it. "The arthritis is . . .", "The cancer is . . .," "The pain is . . ."

Watch your language. Your subconscious mind hears what you say. If you speak of a malady in a possessive way, it is like instructing your body's computer to keep the problem. It's like saying, "This is mine, and I want to keep it."

LETTING EMOTIONS GO

There is a definite connection between emotional health and physical health. If you want to heal your body, you may need to heal your emotions first.

All emotions are essentially good. Emotions are divine. They are simply the energy of our thoughts moving through the body. All emotions are harmless. But when we resist feeling an emotion, when we repress or deny it, the energy doesn't move. The emotion doesn't change. Repressed emotions cause stress and all kinds of physical problems. It is usually not the emotions you know about that hurt your body. It's the emotions you are unconscious of that rob you of vitality.

All addictive and compulsive behavior is an attempt to suppress emotions, to avoid feeling unpleasant feelings. That is why the alcoholic drinks, the addict uses drugs, the smoker lights up, the overeater binges and the compulsive cleaner scrubs clean floors. These are all ways of distracting oneself from a painful emotional reality.

Resistance is painful because the more one tries to escape, the more emotional pain there is. Consider this movie scene: A man phones his wife to say, "I'll be working late tonight." She says, "Again?" as she starts toward the liquor cabinet. She drinks in an attempt to avoid her emotions. She knows her husband is having an affair, but rather than confront him and all of the fear, anger and guilt she feels, she numbs herself with alcohol.

Even when addictions are not present, unexpressed emotions block the flow of life in the mind and body. Releasing emotions is essential to your well-being.

It is easy for God to heal emotions. We cannot heal anything by ourselves, but God can heal everything. Emotions that need releasing will make themselves clear to you. Ask God to show you what you are suppressing. Just pray, "Dear God, if I am denying any emotion, please show me the truth now."

Whatever emotions or realizations occur after you say this prayer will be the very thing you need to be aware of, so pay attention. Do not be afraid to do this exercise. God will not reveal to you more than you can handle.

Releasing emotions requires:
1. Awareness of the emotion.
2. Asking God to heal it.

In her book *A Return to Love*, Marianne Williamson wrote, "We heal through noticing and prayer. Awareness alone does not heal us. If analysis by itself could heal our wounds, we would all be healed by now." Soon after I read that book, I became upset over something that had happened to me and I noticed that I was still angry. I prayed, "Dear God, right now I'm angry but I'm willing to let you take the anger from me." A few minutes later I couldn't remember what I'd been upset about. I was happy. That's how fast and easy it can work for you.

You don't have to know what caused the emotions. Just let them go. Some people get hung up on the idea that they have to know what an emotion is all about before they can release it. No! You don't need to understand your anger, fear or guilt. You need to pray to God to remove those feelings. That is all.

LETTING FEAR GO

The purpose of every experience is to teach you that there is nothing to fear. Gerald G. Jampolsky, M.D., the author of *Teach Only Love,* defines health as inner peace and healing as letting go of fear. Healing is simple. When people come to me for help I know that no matter what outer disease appears to be the problem, the real cause is fear. What they are really trying to heal is fear, not the body.

Fear causes all problems and love solves them all. Fear is the absence of love, as darkness is the absence of light. Darkness is not real. It is not a thing you can chase out of a room. You don't dispel darkness by sweeping it under the rug. You illuminate a dark place by turning on the light. Eliminate fear by turning on love. Love is acceptance. It's okay to feel scared.

Fear has no power in itself. It is only a feeling. It is our resistance to feeling the fear that is the problem. When you allow yourself to feel fear this is what will happen: You feel afraid. That's all. When you allow yourself to feel any emotion, it moves and changes. Fear, once felt, can then become a feeling of excitement, determination, or even joy.

All negative emotions are forms of fear. Guilt is fear of punishment, jealousy is fear of loss, and so on. It's fear that keeps you stuck in unhealthy and unfulfilling situations. It's nothing but plain old fear that keeps you from doing what you really want to do.

Fear is an illusion in your mind. It is not caused by crime, stock market crashes, or atomic bombs. Fear is created by the way we think. It's not what happens, it's our interpretation of what happens, what we think it means. It's only our thoughts that frighten us.

After recording one of my *Success Without Stress*™ tapes, the studio technician said, "It's so nice to hear someone talk about peace. You see so much violence everywhere you go." I thought for a second, "What is he talking about? I don't see any violence." Then I said to him, "Stop watching the news."

He said, "I know the news never really changes but I get so curious as to what's going on."

I asked, "Is there any violence in your personal life?"

He said, "No."

When we watch bad news on television or read about it every day in the newspaper, we start to believe that these problems are really part of our own life. The studio technician thought he lived in a violent world because he watched violence on the screen of a little square box every day.

Fear is an hallucination. It is never based on what is happening now. It is always caused by what we imagine might happen in the future. Finding blood in your urine is not scary in itself. It is frightening only because you tend to imagine the worst possible future.

We can handle anything that is happening in the present moment. The future scares the life out of us. Yet the future is only an illusion in our minds. We have no way of knowing what will happen in the future, or what any experience in the future will be like. We live only in the present.

Suppose you want to go to the store late at night, but you're afraid you might get robbed. What are you really afraid of? You're not scared of what's happening now, but of something you are imagining—in the "future." What if you decide to go to the store and, as you walk outside, a man approaches you, pulls a gun and says, "Give me your wallet." You fear, not the present situation, but your image that he'll shoot you—in a "future" moment.

What if he does shoot you? If you are alive, you are afraid you might die. Again you are not frightened by what is happening now; it is your picture of the future that scares you. Let's say you actually die from the gunshot wound. Now we've reached the ultimate fear, the fear of death.

Death is an illusion, just as fear is an illusion. It's not real. There is no death. The body becomes inanimate, but you are not a body. You are eternal spirit. Death is like the pool of water you see in the road up ahead on a hot summer day. When you get there, the road is dry. The water was just a mirage.

When I first started teaching this course, I phoned a student who had enrolled in the program several months earlier. Her son answered the phone and told me she had died.

I said, "I still owe her a healing treatment. You are welcome to come for the session yourself if you'd like."

This was my worst nightmare come true. I told this woman that God would heal her body and she died. I wondered, What did I do wrong? Before the son came for his appointment, in my imagination I pictured him blaming me for his mother's death. I was actually afraid to meet him because of what I was thinking he might say. My professional ethics wouldn't let me cancel the appointment, so I greeted him with a warm smile when he showed up. I gave him the healing treatment. After the session, he asked me, "What religion are you?"

I said, "I've studied many different religions. I had a spiritual experience when I was twenty-two. I experienced being one with the entire universe and I knew that's what God is."

He sat up straight and said, "I had the same experience, right after my mother died. I knew she was in the most blissful place. Whenever I think about it I feel overwhelming peace."

117

Like the fear of death, my fear of meeting this man proved to be just an illusion. Death is a continuation of life. There is no death. Ask God to show you the truth about death. He will teach you, in a way you can understand, that life is eternal.

James came to see me in late October. He was in tears when he told me he didn't expect to be alive for Christmas. I said, "Well there's no guarantee that I'll be here, either. I could get run over by a truck or something."

"But several doctors have told me my condition is terminal," he informed me.

I said, "Tell me about your life. Do you get along with your family?"

He shared that he did not think very highly of any of his family members, especially his wife. "What do you enjoy doing?" I asked. "What really makes you happy?"

He said, "I really don't have the energy to do much of anything."

"When you had more energy, what did you love to do for fun?"

"I used to love to go fishing," he said. "But it's been a long time since I've gone. I used to go all the time but I can't drive myself to the lake anymore."

"Couldn't you get someone to take you?" I asked.

"My wife won't drive me. She doesn't like fishing."

"Well, I'm sure that there is someone near you who loves to go fishing and who would enjoy your company. Would you like me to pray that God sends you a fishing buddy?" I asked.

He said, "Yes."

We prayed. In less than a week a neighbor invited him to go fishing. He looked like a different man the next time I saw him. He was smiling and happy to be alive. He was making plans to rewire his entire house.

If you want to get well you need to find something more exciting to do with your life than being sick. What could you do right now that would make you happy?

CHAPTER 8

ℋealing Your ℛelationships

RELATIONSHIPS ARE INSTRUMENTS OF HEALING

All encounters with people are divine opportunities for healing. You never meet anyone by accident. Everyone you come in contact with is sent to you by God. This is true of the strangers you pass on the street as well as your closest friends and family members. Relationships are divine healing assignments.

Healing is the purpose of every relationship. God arranges every encounter to teach us to love and forgive one another.

THE HEALING POWER OF COMMUNICATION

Health is a measure of your participation in life. The more you authentically share yourself with others, the more alive you feel. The more you participate with others, the healthier you become. Medical research reveals that cancer patients who participate in support groups live an average of twice as long after diagnosis as those who don't. What is so healing about a support group? Why is it that people who meet once a week with others who have a similar problem and just talk, live years longer than those who don't?

Talking is healing because it is through words and conversation that we express ourselves and share our life with others. Sharing life is what keeps us alive.

WE NEED EACH OTHER

Human companionship is a basic human need. We can only know ourselves in relation to other people. We must have contact with others to thrive. When babies are deprived of physical contact, they can not survive. As adults we have other ways of making contact than just physical touching. We can communicate. Whenever we communicate, what we are really doing is sharing our life. Communication is the essence of relating.

The most dreaded form of punishment for prison inmates is solitary confinement. Human beings can handle any form of abuse better than isolation. Yet we sometimes sentence ourselves to solitary confinement. We cut ourselves off from life by spending too much time alone. When sick, we may not want others to see us looking ill. Yet this is when we most need to accept the love and strength of our family and friends. We may think it is nobler to solve our problems all by ourselves; however, there are times when we just can't do it. We need help.

We may think it is more spiritual to retreat to a solitary way of life. But we need to be with other people if we are to thrive. Even those who devote their lives to meditating on a mountain top don't do it by themselves. They join with other monks, yogis, nuns or priests. There is great power generated when people come together for a common purpose. Two people praying for the same result is at least ten times more effective than one person's prayers. That is why twelve-step groups, such as Alcoholics Anonymous, are so successful. Before alcoholics came together to share their experiences, their strengths and hopes in a spiritual way of life, it was very rare for an alcoholic to get off the bottle.

Today there are many different kinds of support groups available. I encourage people to visit new groups and attend group seminars. The more group encounters I experience, the more I know how much we need each other. There is nothing that compares to the energy and power you receive by being part of a supportive group.

WE ARE ALL RELATED

You are in fact already related to everyone. Kinship is already a given. In spirit you already know everyone intimately, but relating on the human level requires communication. Our relatedness is only meaningful if it is expressed through conversation.

The words you speak create your relationships. Without authentic communication there is no relationship. Cliff told me, "My father and I don't get along very well. I talk to him on the phone but I don't tell him what I really think or how I really feel." I said, "You don't really have a relationship with your father. You're not relating."

I once shared a house with a man named Mike. For six months we were roommates, each with our own busy life. We hardly ever sat down and talked. Several years later I attended a relationship seminar. Mike "just happened" to be in this seminar also. After a couple of days I said to another woman, "I lived in the same house with Mike for six months, but I've learned more about him in the last two days than I did in six months of living under the same roof."

She said, "A relationship is a conversation. If you don't talk, then there is no relationship."

Authentic communication is what a relationship is. Sadly, it is often the people we live with that we share the least of our inner selves with. Just because you share a bed with someone doesn't mean you are relating.

Your ability to communicate with others determines the quality of your life much more than the clothes you wear, the car you drive or anything else. Your ability to speak openly and honestly with others makes you or breaks you in the happiness—and health—departments.

YOU CAN HAVE A RELATIONSHIP WITH ANYONE

Once I realized that a relationship consists of communication, I also understood that I can relate with anyone. All I have to do is talk. You don't have to wait to be introduced to someone you find interesting. Introduce yourself. It's not necessary to wait for others to invite you to spend time with them. You can make the invitation.

Say, "Would you like to go to a movie Friday night?" "You're invited to dinner next Saturday." "Would you like to go for some coffee this afternoon?" The world is full of lonely people waiting for an invitation.

The secret to vitality is to give invitations to others. Lynne, a woman repeating this course for the second time, shared, "You changed my life when you told us, 'You can have a relationship with anyone.' I went out with a man a few times last year. I was hoping it would become a romance but it didn't work out that way. For the last several years I've really had a miserable time at Christmas. I felt especially lonely because I'm single. This year I was thinking maybe I'd skip putting up a tree because it's so difficult to carry it into the house and get it to stand up straight by myself. I remembered what you said about giving invitations and I called this man up and said, 'Would you like to help me decorate my Christmas tree?'

"I was so nervous asking the question, but he said, 'Yes.' It was a pleasure to share the evening with someone. We had fun and it was much easier with his help. He's tall, so it was easy for him to put the angel on top of the tree. I'm glad that I can still be friends with him and enjoy his company."

UPSETS ARE DIVINE

Emotional upsets are sure to occur in every relationship. It is normal for human beings to get upset. At one time I thought I was spiritual enough never to get upset. Then I realized I was just very good at repressing my feelings. Resistance is painful. Physical pain is the body's way of expressing repressed emotional pain. When people complain of physical pain, I ask, "What happened that upset you?" Then they tell me what's really bothering them.

If *you* don't speak up when you are upset, your *body* will. I made house calls for six months for Colleen, a widow in her seventies. Some days she was in such intense pain that she could not move. I'd ask her what happened that upset her and she'd always tell me a story of how someone had mistreated her. I asked her if she told the person how she felt. She always said no, she couldn't.

She didn't express her emotional pain in words, so her body expressed the pain physically. When I persisted in pointing out this connection between her unexpressed emotion and the physical problem, she fired me—very nicely, of course.

Unresolved upsets are a major cause of physical dis-ease. Negative feelings that are unspoken can destroy a beautiful relationship. This is so because if you don't say, "I'm upset," then you are no longer relating. For a relationship to live you have to share yourself authentically.

When I started communicating my upset feelings, I found them precious opportunities for growth. Usually love, respect and understanding for each other is greatly expanded when people voice true feelings in a relationship. It is through sharing our emotions that we really come to know and love one another deeply.

Upset feelings indicate where forgiveness is needed. When you feel upset with a loved one, or dislike someone, it is usually not the present person or situation that is bothering you. Instead they are reminding you of someone else, of some past experience you need to forgive. Upsets occur to show us what needs forgiveness.

Peggy marched up to me after a class and said, "Lenore (another student) is driving me crazy. She repeats herself over and over and she goes on and on with her boring stories. Would you tell her not to repeat herself?"

I said, "Lenore is not bothering me. If you feel upset, you should talk to her yourself."

She said, "I don't want to hurt her feelings."

"Remember how I told you at the first class that whatever is standing in the way of your health will come to your attention during this course?"

"Yes," she said. " I remember."

"Well the way that we sometimes become aware of what needs forgiving is by our emotional reactions. Who does Lenore remind you of?"

"She reminds me of my mother. My mother used to repeat everything just like Lenore does."

I said, "I remember you told me that Lenore has been in several other classes you've taken."

She said, "She's been in the last three classes I took before this one, and she always repeats herself."

"It's no accident that she keeps showing up in your life. God has sent her to you to help you heal. You need to forgive your mother. Lenore is a healing angel, sent by God."

Connie phoned me to inquire about this course. She shared that she had been sick for several years. She said, "I'm really mad at my doctor. I've spent thirty thousand dollars on his treatments and he hasn't helped me."

I said, "One of the things I teach is the importance of forgiving. If you want to recover you will need to forgive your doctor."

Connie came for a private appointment. Again she mentioned her anger toward this physician. She said, "He didn't help me and he wasn't honest with me."

"Who does he remind you of?" I asked.

She said, "He doesn't remind me of anyone."

I said, "*A Course in Miracles* says, 'You're never upset for the reason you think.' It's usually that this person is reminding you of someone else. Who does this doctor remind you of?"

"He doesn't look like anyone I know," she said.

"Who was it in the past who didn't help you and wasn't honest with you?"

"Oh, my stepfather."

"That's who you really need to forgive," I said. "You also need to forgive your doctor."

SHARE YOURSELF

The old saying, "If you can't say something nice then don't say anything at all," can really hurt your relationships and your health. If upsets are not discussed, the relationship is dead. I say, "If you can't say something nice then you'd better say what's true for you." The truth I'm talking about is the truth of your experience. When you tell the truth of your honest feelings, healing happens quickly.

I once let a friend stay at my house while I was on vacation. When I got back, there was a note on my door that said, "THE POOL IS GREEN." When I looked at the pool, I was livid. It was so thick with algae that I could almost walk across it. My friend had not followed my instructions and had even turned off the pump.

He called me a month later to chat. We exchanged a few pleasantries but I didn't really want to keep up the small talk with him. I knew if I didn't tell him how I felt, I'd never want to see him again. I said, "I'm mad at you."

"Why?" he asked, surprised.

I said, "My pool is still green and I have not been able to swim in it. I've spent a fortune trying to clear the water and it's been a real annoyance!"

"I'm sorry," he said. "I value your friendship and I would be willing to pay for half the cost."

I thought, "Wow, it really pays to tell the truth."

Your experience of upset emotions is not the ultimate truth, but sharing your true feelings is the way to get closer to the actual truth, which is always love. Love is the only reality in truth. Your experience is subjective. It is colored by your past, old opinions, beliefs and many other factors. Your interpretations are not necessarily true, but your feelings are your true experience.

Acknowledging and sharing your emotional experience is an act of self love. It is a gift of self-acceptance that you give yourself. This is totally different than blaming. Share your upset feelings in order to repair the damage, not to blame the other person for your feelings.

My parents were divorced when I was seven. I had no communication with my father until I was twenty-six years old. I went to Alabama to visit him several times and he was very pleasant and entertaining. However, I felt like I couldn't really share myself with him. One day I decided that I had to communicate some upset emotions I'd had for a long time. I phoned my father and said, "I want to tell you some things that have been bothering me. It shouldn't matter to me now because it happened a long time ago. I want to share this with you so that I can put the past behind me where it belongs."

I told him, "It was really hard for me growing up without a father. Everyone I met always asked me, 'What does your father do?' and I had to explain the situation. Then they'd always say with pity, 'Oh, that's too bad'."

He said, "I know."

"You do?" I asked, with surprise.

He said, "Yes it was hard for me, too. I never had a father."

I had heard the story before of how my father's mother died when he was only five. His father abandoned him and he was raised by neighbors. I'd never really thought about how he would have felt.

He was so understanding and nice. After we talked I felt completely different.

I WANT TO TALK WITH YOU

When you are upset, it is wise to ask the other person to sit down and talk with you rather than trying to resolve a problem while they are busy doing something else, like cooking dinner. If they are unable to sit down with you right away, you can set a time when you can both focus on the conversation.

The best way to start is to say, "I feel ...." I feel angry. I feel hurt. I feel disappointed. I feel sad. I feel confused. You could also say, "When you _____, I felt _____." When you didn't call, I felt scared. When you hugged him, I felt jealous. When you left, I felt lonely.

People do not know what you feel unless you tell them. When you say, "I feel ....," you are communicating heart to heart with another human being who has all of the same emotions that you do. There is tremendous healing power in just saying what you feel to another person. To say, "I feel ....," opens the way for honest sharing for both parties.

On the other hand, if you start the conversation with the word "you," the natural response will be for the other person to defend themselves. They will feel threatened by statements such as, "You hurt my feelings," or "You made me mad." When you start with the word "you", you are not sharing your feelings. What you are doing is blaming the other person for your feelings. You are attacking them.

Others are not responsible for your feelings. No one can make you feel anything. Therefore, statements which start with "you" are not true. The listener will feel attacked when you begin with the energy of blame. No one can be healed in an attack-defend conversation because no real communication is going on. No one is really saying how they truly feel.

Blame is the road to misery. It never does any good to blame someone else for your unhappiness, yet it is tempting to do so because to say, "I feel ....," is to expose a part of yourself that is vulnerable. It is scary to be so open.

It is impossible to avoid being vulnerable. Real honest communication is not possible without revealing your vulnerable underbelly, and it is this soft, vulnerable part of you that makes you really lovable. It is the sharing of these tender emotions that evokes love in others.

EMOTIONAL HONESTY IS EMOTIONAL HEALTH

We all start life with total honesty. Children are emotionally honest. They have no problem making their needs known and expressing their true feelings. Children cry and laugh. They fight with one another and make up five minutes later. They sing and dance and make noise. Children are full of life. They simply express themselves.

Adults marvel at the sight of spontaneous little people. "How can they have so much energy?" we wonder. "Was I ever that deliriously joyful?"

Yes, you were! There was a time when you made no judgments. You simply loved life and you held nothing back. The joy and exuberance of youth returns as you begin to share yourself openly with others. The more you say what you really think and express what you really feel, the more others will love you.

It is ironic that we hold back our true thoughts and feelings for fear of being rejected, yet unless we can share the tender, defenseless part of ourselves, there is not much visible for another to love.

The most lovable thing about you is your faults. My friend Almon Eastman told me, "People love you when you tell them your faults. They feel safe with you." It is hard to love someone who doesn't share their less than perfect side.

Health is emotional freedom. An emotionally healthy individual can respond genuinely to the present situation without blaming. They can communicate so that they get what they want and need.

More than ninety percent of all illness is caused by stress, but what is stress? Different things are stressful to different people. I define stress as *the inability to respond to life*. For example, let's say I go to a doctor's office and I have to wait two hours in the waiting room. I'm feeling angry, but I don't say anything because I think it's not nice to be angry. This is stressful because some "should" in my head is preventing me from relating to life in an honest, authentic way.

Eliminate the word "should" from your vocabulary. Rather than ask yourself, "What should I do?" ask, "What do I want?"

ASK PEOPLE FOR WHAT YOU WANT

I was bedridden for a year following an automobile collision. Every morning I got up thinking, "I'm going to work today." But by the time I was dressed, I was exhausted. I had to go back to bed. I didn't have the energy to cook, so I ate cookies and other junk food. This diet didn't help my energy level at all. I needed someone to help me with my meals but I didn't ask anyone to do so. I lived alone. I often thought that if someone would just lie down beside me and hold me, I'd feel better. But I never once asked anyone to do that.

I thought no one cared about me. There was no one to help me. I'd always been "Joanna-on-the-spot" to help my friends when they were sick. Many times I had offered my help without being asked, but no one showed up for me like that.

Finally I dragged myself to a seminar on communication. The question was asked, "What's your act?"

I said, "I don't have an act. I'm fine." Those very words were my act. I always said, "I'm fine," no matter what was going on. When people asked, "How are you?" I said, "I'm fine." After some time I realized that my friends didn't know what I needed because I didn't tell them. The painful truth was, I would rather have died than ask for help.

Seeing clearly that this didn't work, I made a commitment to ask for help and I started asking people for what I wanted and needed.

I found that my friends were delighted to assist me and I got better quickly. I also stopped rushing in to help others before they asked for my help.

What is it you'd rather die than do?

MAKE REQUESTS

Nancy said, "He's so selfish, he didn't even offer to pick me up at the airport!"

"Did you ask him to do that?" I wanted to know.

She said, "No."

Like Nancy, many of us would rather complain than get what we want. It is emotionally safer to blame others than to take responsibility for our relationships working.

Learning to make requests has been a real school of personal growth for me. It took me several years to really become skilled in the art of making requests. Now it seems very simple and easy for me, but that was not always so. The trouble was I had too much attachment to whether or not people said yes. I wanted the answer to be "Yes" so badly that I could not emotionally risk the possibility of them saying "No." It was safer not to make the request—but then I didn't have any chance of getting what I wanted!

My business coach, Dwight GoldWinde, helped me break this losing cycle of not making requests. He created a different game. He suggested that I make one request every day and reward myself for doing so whether or not the answer was "Yes."

I started by saying things like, "I'm going to ask you a favor, but if you don't want to do it, that's O.K." I kept records of my "Yes" and "No" responses and I was surprised to find that I got a "Yes" answer to more than eighty percent of my requests.

ASK AGAIN

Once I was upset and I wanted someone to come to my home and comfort me. I called my best friend Louisa. She wasn't home. I called another friend, and she wasn't home either. I thought, "No one is ever around when I need them." I started journaling about my feelings and I decided I was going to call everyone I knew until someone came to comfort me. The next couple I phoned, Linda and Tom, came right over to support me. They were wonderful.

Getting what you want is your responsibility. Stop complaining and start making requests. Keep asking for what you want and need. If one person says "No," ask someone else.

A good way of wording a request is to say, "I have a request of you." Then ask for what you want. The word *request* communicates that you are not making a demand. Most people will happily honor your request if they can.

Some people spend a lot of time communicating their feelings or their problems but then they forget to make a request. When you want to resolve an upset, it is good to start the conversation with "I feel _____," and end with "I request _____." "I feel unhappy that the dinner is overcooked, and I request that you call me the next time you are going to be late." "I feel sad, and I would like you to hug me." "I feel upset, so please set aside Sunday afternoon to talk with me."

During the part of the course when I teach my students to listen to their body, a woman said, "I asked my body what I need to do in order to heal the pain in my shoulder. My body said, 'Stop lifting the watermelons.' I work as a cashier in a supermarket and I have to lift big heavy watermelons out of the cart for people all day."

"Why don't you ask them to do it?" I asked.

She said "I do, but they tell me they can't. I feel like saying, 'How did you get it in there if you can't pick it up?' but I go ahead and strain myself by leaning over the basket and lifting it out."

I said, "I don't know what the solution to your problem is but I know there is a solution. Ask God for the perfect solution." After the conversation about making requests, this woman raised her hand and said, "I didn't lift a single watermelon this week and everyone had them in their carts because we were having a big sale."

"What did you do?" I wanted to know.

She said, "I asked the men to pick them up for me."

"So you were asking your female customers before?" I asked?

"Yes, but this week I asked the men. I'd say to any man nearby, 'Would you please pick this up for me?' They were so macho. They were delighted that I wanted their help. They really enjoyed doing me a favor. If there were no men around, I asked a carryout person to lift it for me. My shoulder sure feels better."

ASK AGAIN AND AGAIN

If you keep asking for what you want you are sure to get it. When you get a "No," don't get mad, just ask someone else or ask again at another time. Be grateful for the honesty when someone says "No" to your request. "No" just means, "It's not appropriate for me at this time." You will receive what you want in the flow of life. Don't push the river. When you ask the right person at the right time, it will be perfect for everyone. Keep asking.

YOU HAVE TO TRAIN PEOPLE TO TREAT YOU
THE WAY YOU WANT TO BE TREATED

Bill White, who teaches a seminar called *Communicating Through Upsets,* says, "You have to teach people how to win with you."

Joyce said, "This week I received a phone call that made me very sad. One of my best friends died. When I hung up the phone I started crying. My two grown sons were sitting right there and I thought, 'Somebody please hug me,' but they didn't. Are you saying I should have asked them for a hug?"

"Yes. If you had said, 'I need a hug,' I'll bet they both would have put their arms around you. You have to tell people what you want and need because they don't know. Your sons literally didn't know what to do. They needed a request from you."

Here is the main rule in getting what you want and need from others: IF YOU ARE NOT GETTING THE RESPONSE YOU WANT, DO SOMETHING DIFFERENT. Try a different tone of voice, different words or gestures. Don't keep doing the same thing. If you've tried yelling and screaming and that didn't work, try a different way of communicating. Lower the volume and make a clear, calm request. On the other hand if you've tried being patient and nice and you are not getting what you want, experiment with a louder voice. See what happens when you stomp your foot or shake your fist.

A student named Bob said, "For the last eighteen years, whenever my wife and I had a heated conversation, I did most of the talking. I thought it was my job to keep the conversation going. This week we got into an argument but, instead of doing what I usually do, I kept seeing the words from the class handout, 'TRY SOMETHING DIFFERENT.' So I let her talk and I listened. It was amazing. I discovered things about her and myself that I didn't know. In all these years I had never tried listening to her."

What is it you keep doing over and over, even though it doesn't work?

BALANCE IS HEALTHY

Life has a way of teaching us balance. Anything that is taken to the extreme is unhealthy. If you are extremely independent you may find yourself surrounded by people who are extremely dependent. Relationship problems are one of the ways God guides us to more balanced behavior.

Rigid patterns of thinking and reacting bring painful lessons to the degree that we are inflexible. No rigid way of living will bring health and happiness.

Many of the books I've read on spiritual healing say, "Stop talking about your ailments." Some say, "Never talk about your problems. Take your mind off the problem and it will disappear." For many people it is good medicine to follow this advice. However, some individuals need to learn to share their problems with others. These people suffer in silence. They miss out on the support that others could give them. If the way you are relating to others is not bringing you the love and peace you want, why not experiment with new behaviors?

THE HEALING POWER OF TOUCH

Laura was having difficulties with her feet. She could barely walk and she was upset that she was not able to participate with her three children as she wanted.

"Get your kids to massage your feet," I told her.

She said, "It's hard for me to ask for that kind of support."

"They'll enjoy it if you are patient with them," I said. "Kids have enormous healing energy. I once went to the home of a massage therapist to give the therapist a healing treatment. When I got there she was on her massage table, instructing her seven-year-old grandson on how she liked to be massaged. Children want to contribute to your well-being, but you have to teach them how and show appreciation for their efforts."

She started asking her children to massage her feet every day. Immediately her feet felt better, and soon she was walking normally.

Human touch is an essential part of a healthy life. When I first heard that you need eight hugs a day to stay healthy, I thought, "I'm lucky if I get even one." I decided to start asking for hugs. At first I was afraid of being rejected, but everyone I asked was happy to give me a hug. I started asking my patients, my friends and my co-workers for hugs. What a difference it made!

If you have pain, ask a friend to massage the affected area for you. You can always return the favor. Everyone wins. Headaches, tummy aches and many common discomforts can be banished or at least lessened through gentle rubbing or stroking.

When I speak at nursing homes, I encourage the patients to massage each other. All animals groom or massage each other as a natural part of their existence, but sometimes we sophisticated humans forget to do likewise. We may be afraid to reach out to another, but we have nothing to lose and a lot to gain.

A friend offered to massage my feet one day and I said, "No, thanks, I'm too busy." Then I changed my mind and said O.K. As I received his kindness, I realized how much love I reject or turn away. There is no shortage of love. It is only our unwillingness to receive love that makes us think love is scarce.

ASK OTHERS TO PRAY FOR YOU

Prayer is the most powerful support you could give to or receive from another person. Ask your friends to pray for you. You might simply say, "Would you pray for my health and healing?"

One Sunday I woke up with a strange dizziness. I was scheduled to give a sermon about healing that day and I was concerned that I might fall or trip in the pulpit. For the first time I asked my roommate to pray for me. We prayed out loud and I was instantly much better. I did the service with no dizziness and it never returned.

"Why should we wait until there's a problem before praying together?" I thought. We decided to make a habit of praying out loud together every week.

There is a Prayer for a Partner located in appendix D, page 177.

BE GENEROUS WITH COMMUNICATION

Barbara was having trouble with her live-in lover. She said, "I can't go to the party because I told John I'd stay home with him. I wish I hadn't said that. Now, if I change my mind, he'll be angry."

I said, "If you made an agreement to stay home, then that is what you should do. Keeping your word is what a relationship is all about."

Barbara said, "Do you really think so?"

"Oh, yes," I said. "It doesn't matter what the agreement is. The important thing in a relationship is keeping your word. Do what you said you would do and the relationship will work out."

If you say you are going to do something, do it. Every time you break your word, you hurt your self-esteem. When you act as if your word doesn't mean anything, you lose respect for yourself.

When you are not going to fulfill an agreement, it is wise to let the other party know as soon as possible. Most of our relationship problems are caused by our failure to communicate. Any honest communication is a gift, even if it is bad news. The truth is always healing. Speak it generously.

YOUR INTENTION

The words you communicate are only about twenty percent of the message your listener receives. Your tone of voice, facial expressions and body language say much more than your words. When you put them all together, what you communicate most effectively is your intention.

If your intention is to clear the air and restore the relationship to harmony, this will come through in your choice of words as well as your tone of voice and body language.

When I have a difficult communication to deliver, I sometimes become overly concerned with the words. "How can I put this?" It is a big help for me to say a prayer. I ask God to help me, and then I start talking.

ACKNOWLEDGE YOURSELF FOR GROWING

Breaking old, limiting programming about the right way to relate is a healthy step. Always applaud yourself for expressing your truth, even if the results are not spectacular. Acknowledge yourself even if your communication or your feelings are awkward. Personal growth feels scary and uncomfortable because it means sailing into uncharted waters. That is OK. The truth will always guide you safely home to Love.

TALK TO THE RIGHT PERSON

If you complain to a third party about something someone did or said, you are talking to the wrong person. When you are upset, talk directly to the person who evoked the upset emotions. He or she is the one who can heal you best.

It does no good and much harm to complain to others, yet it is an easy habit to develop. If you find yourself gossiping or complaining to a third party about someone who isn't there to respond, stop immediately and contact the right person.

Refuse to engage in the gossip of others. Make a commitment to defend those who are absent.

HOW TO SAY NO

Do you say "Yes" when you want to say "No"? That is a common problem. Ann told me that she could not say "No" to her grown children. She routinely spent more than she had in order to buy them things they requested. I thought about her situation and said, "No wonder you experience trouble. I find it hard to say 'No,' too. I say, 'That doesn't work for me'." For some reason it's easier to say no if you use different words, such as, "I appreciate your offer, but I've decided to decline."

Others have the freedom to say "No" to your requests. You also have the right to say "No." I used to think that if someone made a request of me, I had to say yes or no right then. Now I know that I don't have to make an immediate decision. It's O.K. to say, "I'll think about it and call you tomorrow." This statement allows plenty of time to think it over and ask for divine guidance.

The purpose of this chapter is to encourage you to participate with others in new ways. It is not intended to tell you everything there is to know about relating to others. I'm simply sharing some information that has been helpful to me. Everyone has different lessons to learn about relating to people. You may be one of those people who find it easy to say no but difficult to say yes. While writing this chapter I realized that every important spiritual experience I've ever had involved the help—or at least the presence—of one or more other human beings.

"I LOVE YOU"

These are the words at the heart of all communications: I LOVE YOU. Can you speak these simple words of affection? Can you say, "Thank you"? How often do you speak words of love and appreciation?

Some folks find it easy to express upset emotions, but difficult to express tender, loving feelings.

Numerous parents told me that their biggest mistake in parenting was withholding approval from their children. Approval is a wonderful emotion, but even positive feelings can be painful if they are not expressed. When we lose a loved one, it is the "I love you's" we didn't say that hurt the most.

Paul lost his brother. He shared that he had no regrets regarding his brother. He said, "We always said, 'I love you,' before we said goodbye on the phone or in person."

I unexpectedly saw my friend Bill Attaway at a outdoor cafe. He invited me to sit with him. I pulled up a chair and said, "I have to tell you I love you so much. I think you are wonderful."

He said, "I love you, too." Then after a long silence he added, "I was speaking on a television talk show last week. I said, you can tell how enlightened you are by the number of people you say I love you to."

It is easy to assume that our dear ones know that we love them by the many thoughts we have of them. But they can't hear our thoughts. Let them hear the sweetest words of all: "I love you."

CHAPTER 9

Finding The Right Healer For You

George asked me, "Do you think we should go to doctors, or do you believe we can just heal ourselves?"

I said, "I think it's a big mistake to think we can always heal ourselves. There are times when we should go to a doctor or other healer. It could be an M.D., a psychologist, a nutritionist or just someone to talk to. There are times when we need other people to help us." God designed this world so that we need each other. *Your health can not be maintained by you alone.*

There are so many types of healers in the world: medical doctors, counselors, psychologists, psychiatrists, chiropractors, massage therapists, spiritual healers and a thousand others. How do you know which one to go to?

You will know when you meet the right healer for you. How will you know? You will just know. You may see their picture in an ad and feel attracted to them. You may hear a friend tell you of their experience with a doctor or other healer and definitely sense you want to experience that person yourself.

If more than one person tells me about someone, I consider that a sign to try them. But if one person tells me about a healer and I get excited, that also is a signal to go see them. These are the gentle proddings of God's guidance.

The next step is to meet the healer. Call them for an appointment. Your divine healer will usually do or say something that will make you feel better right away. Some people put off seeing a doctor, dentist or other healer, because they are afraid that it won't do any good. I think it is better to give a doctor a chance and see how you feel. Notice how you are treated. Are you regarded with kindness and compassion? Do you get a good feeling from this person? If not, then don't go back.

When you *take action* to find healing, God gets the message that you are serious about being well and sends you more guidance. Do not get discouraged if you visit several healers who are not right for you. No matter what the problem, there is someone who can help you overcome it.

YOUR TRUE HEALER WILL BE AFFORDABLE

At one time I found myself in a great deal of emotional pain and confusion. I realized I needed help. I prayed for guidance and someone told me about a wonderful rebirther. I didn't have the money to pay for this healing service. My finances were the main reason I was depressed, so I called the rebirther and asked if he would be willing to trade services. He said no. Then someone told me of a fantastic astrologer who did trades, so I called her. She said no. A few days later I received a notice in the mail that one of my favorite spiritual authors, William Samuel, was going to be in town. I called for more information. He worked on a love offering basis. He was doing two lectures and scheduling private sessions during his visit. I prayed, "Thank you, God."

On hearing William Samuel speak, I had a healing of my attitude—and a breakthrough in my finances soon followed. I also became personal friends with my favorite author. When you find your divine healer, the money will work out one way or another. Either the healer will be willing to take time payments or you will receive the money to pay for the service. One way or another the money will be provided.

Ask about prices and possible payment options. If additional treatments are suggested, ask about the cost. You have the right to ask questions. If money is a concern, ask about financial assistance, special payment arrangements and so on.

Noreen had a lump in her breast. She went to a doctor who took x-rays and scheduled her for surgery. Noreen did not have the money to pay the deductible on her insurance. She told me, "I stayed up all night praying for God to heal me and to provide a way for me to pay the doctor bills. When I went in for the surgery the next day, the doctor decided to take another x-ray. He looked at it and told me to go home. There was some kind of mistake before and now I didn't need surgery." Her sister called the same day and said she was sending her a gift of a thousand dollars.

GOD HEALS US THROUGH OTHER PEOPLE

Your healer is close. There are amazing healers near you now. We tend to think that the really great spiritual healers or teachers are far away in India or the Orient. It has been my experience that miracle performing healers are everywhere. When you pray for God to guide you to them you will find that a truly gifted healer works down the road from you.

The way that God answers our prayers is often through other people. God heals us with the help of a doctor, the love of a friend and the words of others. Pray for God to send you the right healer and be open to accept help from others.

Pray: "Dear God, please send the perfect healer to me right away. I know there is someone out there who can heal me. I am open and ready to accept help now. Thank you, God."

CHAPTER 10

The Six Week Healing Program

"I ALREADY KNOW THIS STUFF, SO WHY AM I STILL SICK?"

A beautiful woman came up to me after a class and said, "I already know this stuff, but I do need some help."

As I drove home, I thought about her comment and marveled at what a left-brain, logical orientation we have to everything. We think knowledge is all we need. But information without action is worthless. What you *know* will not improve the quality of your life very much. It's what you *do* with the knowledge that makes the difference.

While browsing in a bookstore, I picked up *The Abundance Book* by John Randolph Price. Glancing through it, I told myself, "I already know this." I put the book back on the shelf. Six months later I saw the same book in another bookstore. This time I bought it. Reading the book, I thought again, "This information is not new to me."

The book included a forty-day prosperity program with specific instructions to follow every day. I made a commitment to follow the plan and I did exactly what the directions said to do each and every day for forty days. On the forty-fifth day, I received a check for twenty thousand dollars. This experience taught me the value of taking what I know and applying it for a specific period of time.

One of the most valuable things I've learned is the tremendous power of repetition. We can only integrate new ideas into our daily life by repetition. After church, I often purchase a recording of the sermon and listen to it in the car all week. It is amazing how much "new" information I hear during the sixth and seventh listening. Was I asleep in church?

No. It's just that we can absorb only so much useful information at one time. It takes time and repetition to change. That is why you need to do this six-week healing program. It will help you put these powerful techniques into practice as part of your daily life.

You may modify the program to fit your schedule and your needs. This six week healing program can be done alone, with a prayer partner, or as part of a support group. Having a prayer partner or support group will make it easier for you to receive encouragement and assistance If you are interested in starting a support group, you may request a free packet of information that will help you get started. (There is a one dollar charge for shipping.)

THIS IS FUN !

Doing these daily assignments will be a delightful pleasure once you get into the rhythm. Rather than making it another chore, think of it as play. You are learning fun, new skills. You are taking the time to love and heal yourself.

Stick with the program for the entire six weeks even if it feels awkward at first. Many fun activities are not fun in the beginning. When I first started skiing, I fell down dozens of times. But once I got the hang of it, skiing was immensely joyful. Writing this book was the same way. At first it was torture for me to sit down and write the things I so often say. Yet, after a few weeks of writing for an hour every day, I began to look forward to it. I felt such excitement that I didn't want to stop when the hour was up.

When you take the time to love yourself and care for your body, everything else will take care of itself. Donna had a cyst on her uterus. She and her doctors were afraid that it might be malignant. She received this six-week healing program and decided to do it even though she was extremely busy. She had been trying for months to save two failing companies. Both her own business and her husband's were in serious financial trouble. In fact, his company was in such trouble that he had been unable to pay himself or his employees for some time.

A friend asked Donna how the six-week healing program was going. She said, "I really like it but it takes so much time."

Her friend asked, "But, what's more important than your health?" She stuck with the program and by the sixth week the cyst had completely disappeared. During that time, both of their businesses had turned around dramatically. They were prospering.

HOMEPLAY FOR WEEK NUMBER 1

1. Reread Chapter 1, The Healing Power of Prayer, and Chapter 2, The Healing Power of Love.

2. Every day, pray for at least five minutes the very first thing in the morning. Send God's Love ahead of you every morning. See page 175.

3. Each evening before you go to sleep, spend at least five minutes in prayer. Send God's Love ahead of you into your dream time.

4. Make a list of fifty or more things you like about your body and yourself. This is an average of eight per day.

5. Either purchase the *God Will Heal Your Body* tape or record the Healing Relaxation Tape script on page 169. Listen to this tape once each day this week.

6. Tape the affirmation of the week onto your bathroom mirror, page 179.

HOMEPLAY FOR WEEK NUMBER 2

1. Reread Chapters 3 and 4, Affirmations, and The Healing Power of Relaxation, pages 41-56.

2. Listen to your tape once each day.

3. Practice the Relaxation Prayer on page 54 once every day.

4. Write your personal affirmation ten times every day. Speak it aloud ten times.

5. Continue to send God's Love every morning and every night.

6. Put the affirmation of the week, located on page 179, somewhere you will see it often.

HOMEPLAY FOR WEEK NUMBER 3

1. Reread Chapter 5, Listen to Your Body, page 57.

2. Practice listening to your body at least once every day.

3. Listen to your tape once daily.

4. Do the Relaxation Prayer once each day, page 54.

5. Write your personal affirmation ten times every day. Recite it aloud each time you write it.

6. Continue sending God's Love every morning and evening.

7. Put the affirmation of the week where you will see it often, page 180.

HOMEPLAY FOR WEEK NUMBER 4

1. Reread Chapter 6, Forgiveness, The Heart of Healing, page 75.

2. Make a list of everyone you need to forgive starting from your childhood. Include everything you need to forgive yourself for.

3. Pick a forgiveness affirmation and write it ten to seventy times every day this week.

4. Listen to your tape once each day.

5. Practice the Relaxation Prayer on page 54 once every day.

6. Write your personal affirmation ten times every day. Say it out loud ten times.

7. Send God's Love ahead of you every morning and every night.

8 Use the affirmation of the week, page 180.

HOMEPLAY FOR WEEK NUMBER 5

1. Burn or bury your forgiveness affirmations and your forgiveness list, releasing everyone on it to their divine good.

2. Reread Chapter 7, Letting Go, page 99.

3. Go through your entire house and throw out, sell or give away everything you no longer want or use. If you need help with this project, ask others to assist you. If you can't do the entire house this week, set a date by which you will finish the task. Complete at least one room this week.

4. Listen to your tape once every day.

5. Write your personal affirmation ten times. Speak it aloud ten times.

6. Practice the Relaxation Prayer on page 54 once each day.

7. Write the affirmation for releasing, "I, (your name), am now willing to release everything and everyone that is no longer for my highest good."

6. Send God's Love ahead of you every morning and every night.

7. Use the affirmation of the week, page 181.

HOMEPLAY FOR WEEK NUMBER 6

1. Reread Chapter 8, Healing Your Relationships, page 121, and Chapter 9, Finding the Right Healer for You, page 149.

2. Listen to your tape every day.

3. Practice the Relaxation Prayer on page 54 every day.

4. Write your personal affirmation ten times every day. Say your affirmation aloud ten times.

5. Send God's Love ahead of you each morning and night.

6. Tape the affirmation of the week where you will read it often, page 181.

SHARE YOUR EXPERIENCE

When you've completed the six-week healing program please write me and share your experience. Tell me what your condition was before you began the program, and the results you've noticed.

Share your experience with your friends. The only way to keep your spiritual awareness alive is by sharing it with others. When you tell another human being about the big or small miracles you've received, you prepare yourself to accept more miracles. You open the door for your next insight. The more you share your spiritual experiences with others, the more aware of God's presence you become.

APPENDIX A

HEALING AFFIRMATIONS

Personalize these affirmations so that you have the words that describe the exact result you want. You do not need to use all of the sentences that are written here. Choose one or two statements that appeal to you emotionally.

FOR MORE ENERGY

I am full of vim and vigor. I have pep and energy. I, (your name), am enthusiastic about life and living. I have get up and go. I am a go-getter. I love my life. My energy is increasing more and more every day.

FOR MORE MONEY

I open my mind to an understanding of the all providing love of God. I am God's beloved child. I am worthy of financial riches because of who I am. My Father is the biggest tycoon in the universe. I deserve great sums of money. Money is good. I am open to receive all of the goodness and all of the money that God has for me. Money comes to me easily and abundantly now. My every need is met. Through God's Love within me, I am able to honor all of my financial commitments. I rejoice that God is continuously providing more than enough money to pay every bill on time. Every dollar I give out circulates, enriches the economy and comes back to me multiplied. I trust God to provide for me abundantly now. Money now comes to me more abundantly, easily and joyfully than ever before. My income is increasing.

FOR BETTER SLEEP

I now fall asleep easily. I sleep peacefully throughout the entire night. My dreams are all pleasant. I sleep well every night and I wake up refreshed every morning.

FOR YOUTH

I am young! I feel young. I look young. I think like a youth. I am becoming more and more youthful every day.

FOR REDUCING WEIGHT

I am naturally slender and energetic. I am now thin and beautiful (or handsome). I am sustained by God's Love. I feel light and happy.

FOR HEALING CONSTIPATION

My bowels are moving easily, naturally and regularly. My elimination system functions perfectly now. I relax and let go of the past. It is safe to release what my body no longer needs.

FOR HEALING FEAR

I am safe right now. All is well. Everything happens for the best. God is with me. I am always safe.

FOR HEALING THE SKIN

My skin is clear, smooth and beautiful. My skin looks young and healthy. The skin on my _____ is healthy and normal now. My skin feels good. I am safe.

FOR HEALING THE MIND

I am at peace now. My mind is full of God's infinite intelligence and health. I think clearly now. My mind is alert and clear. My brain is functioning perfectly now. I am happy and healthy. My mind is open to the idea of perfect health.

FOR HEALING THE EYES

My vision is now 20/20. My eyes are perfect and healthy. My vision is perfect. I see clearly now. My eyes are relaxed. I look at life with loving eyes and I see the truth very well. My eyes are well. I thank God for my perfect eyes.

FOR HEALING THE EARS

My ears are open and receptive to hear the truth. I hear perfectly well now. I am balanced and healthy. I hear the beauty of all sounds now. My ears feel good.

FOR HEALING THE NOSE

I breath easily and deeply now. My nose is healthy and well. My nose is beautiful and perfect. My sense of smell is perfect. My nose feels good.

FOR HEALING THE MOUTH

My mouth is now healthy. My lips and teeth and gums are beautiful, healthy and strong. I like the taste of life. My mouth feels good.

FOR HEALING THE THROAT

I voice my thoughts clearly and easily. My throat is healthy and normal now. It is safe for me to speak the truth. My throat feels good.

FOR HEALING THE NECK

My neck is flexible, strong and relaxed. My neck is normal and healthy. My neck feels good.

FOR HEALING THE SHOULDERS

My shoulders are now healthy and beautiful. My shoulders are flexible and strong. My shoulders are relaxed. My shoulders feel good.

FOR HEALING THE ARMS

My arms are now healthy and well. I can easily move my arms in every direction. My joints are healthy and normal now. My arm muscles, ligaments and tendons are normal. My arms feel good.

FOR HEALING THE HANDS

My hands are now perfectly healthy. My hands and fingers are flexible. I let go now and trust in the goodness of God. My hands are well. My hands feel good.

FOR HEALING THE LUNGS

My lungs are now clean and clear and beautiful. I breath in new life with each breath. My lungs are healthy now. My lungs are normal and well. My lungs feel good.

FOR HEALING THE HEART

My heart is strong and fit. My heart is perfectly well now. My heartbeat is normal and healthy. My arteries are clear. My circulation is working perfectly now. I have a healthy, loving heart. My heart feels good.

FOR HEALING THE BREASTS

My breasts are beautiful and healthy. Both of my breasts are perfect. I nurture myself and others with love. My breasts are healthy and well. My breasts look and feel good.

FOR HEALING THE STOMACH

My stomach is healthy and well. My stomach works beautifully. My digestion is perfect. My stomach is calm and peaceful. I have a normal, healthy stomach. I love my wonderful stomach. My stomach feels good.

FOR HEALING THE PANCREAS

My life is sweet and wonderful. My pancreas is healthy now. My blood sugar is normal. I have vim and vigor and pep. I feel vital and alive.

FOR HEALING THE SPLEEN

My spleen is healthy and strong now. My spleen is strong and well. I feel safe and secure.

FOR HEALING THE LIVER

I have a fine healthy liver. My liver is strong. My liver is normal. My liver is now working perfectly. I am well.

FOR HEALING THE INTESTINES

My digestive system is working perfectly now. I easily assimilate and digest food. My intestines are healthy and strong now. I feel good.

FOR HEALING THE COLON

My colon is healthy and beautiful. My bowels are working perfectly now. My colon eliminates all that is not needed by my body, and I am filled with vitality.

FOR HEALING THE KIDNEYS

Both of my kidneys are strong and healthy. My kidneys are functioning perfectly and easily. I feel wonderful.

FOR HEALING THE BLADDER

My bladder is healthy and normal. I have a beautiful, perfect bladder. I feel great now.

FOR HEALING THE GENITALS

My genitals (vagina, uterus, ovaries, penis, or testicles) are healthy now. My reproductive system is healthy. My sexuality is a healthy and important part of my life. I accept myself as a sexual being. I feel healthy and strong.

FOR HEALING THE LEGS

My thighs, knees and legs are strong and healthy. I walk with confidence. My legs are fit and firm now. I have beautiful legs. My legs look and feel wonderful.

FOR HEALING THE FEET

My feet are healthy and strong. I stand and walk easily now. My feet support my body perfectly. I thank God for my understanding of life.

APPENDIX B

THE HEALING RELAXATION TAPE SCRIPT

Either ask a friend to read and record the following script to you as you close your eyes and relax, or you can record it yourself. Change the script from the word "You" to "I" if you record it for yourself. Personalize it by filling in your name and personal affirmation. Be sure to choose a quiet time and place to make this recording and speak very slowly.

Close your eyes, (*your name*), and focus your full attention on the sound of my voice. Just listen to what I am saying. If you find yourself thinking of other things during this session, just bring your full attention back to what I'm saying and don't even stop to scold yourself. You are going to enter a deep, deep, state of physical and mental relaxation, but you will remain awake and alert. You will hear every word that I say.

God always answers your prayers for healing. Take a moment now to ask God for help or healing. In your own way, ask God for help.

(*pause*)

Now use your good imagination and imagine a relaxing power, relaxing the toes of your right foot. Feel the relaxing power in the ball of your right foot, in the arch, and in the heel now. Feel the relaxing power moving up into your ankle now, relaxing completely, relaxing completely. Imagine the relaxing power moving up your leg to your knee, relaxing all of the muscles as it goes, and moving into your thigh muscles now. Relaxing completely, relaxing completely.

Feel the relaxing power now, in the toes of your left foot. Feel this relaxing power moving into the ball, the arch and into your heel. All the way up into your ankle. Limp, limp, loose, loose, completely relaxed, completely relaxed. Now, feel the relaxing power moving up your leg to your knee, relaxing every cell and every atom, and moving into your thigh muscles, all the way up to your hip. Now your entire leg is completely relaxed, completely relaxed.

You feel yourself turning loose completely, both physically and mentally now as the relaxing power relaxes the fingers of your right hand. Relaxing completely. Now into the fingers of your left hand. Relaxing completely. Just allow your arms to relax. Your right forearm is relaxing now. And your left forearm is relaxing. The upper part of your right arm is relaxing completely now. The upper part of your left arm is relaxing completely now. Both of your arms are dangling loosely and comfortably from your shoulders. Completely relaxed. Completely relaxed.

Now you're going to relax the rest of your body by taking three deep slow breaths. As you let these breaths out, your body will relax all over in every way. Also, as you let these breaths out your mind becomes very peaceful and very calm. All right, number one, a deep slow breath in........ and out....... Number two, a deeper breath, in.... and out....... Number three, a very deep breath, in.......

and out........ Complete relaxation is now yours. Your body is deeply relaxed and your mind is very peaceful and very calm.

Now imagine that the relaxing power is relaxing the muscles in the back of your neck and your shoulders. The muscles in the back of your neck and your shoulders are getting very loose and limp, loose and limp, loose and limp.

Feel the relaxing power moving up over your scalp. Relaxing your scalp completely, and pouring down into your eyes. Relaxing all the little muscles around your eyes, and relaxing all of your facial muscles. Limp, limp, loose, loose, completely relaxed, completely relaxed. Let your jaw relax now. Let there be a little space between your teeth.

Feel the relaxing power flowing down into your throat now. All of the muscles in your throat are becoming very soft and relaxed, loose and relaxed. Now you are relaxed all over in every way. Every muscle in your body is loose and limp. Your mind is relaxed and filled with peace. You are very deeply relaxed now, but I want you to relax even more, so I'm going to count backwards from seven to one. When I get to the number one you will be extremely relaxed. You will be much, much more deeply relaxed than you are now, and you will be more deeply relaxed than you have ever been.

Number seven (*pause*). Number six (*pause*). Number five (*pause*). Number four (*pause*). Number three (*pause*). Number two (*pause*) Number one.

Now you are extremely relaxed. Your body is relaxed. Your mind is still and calm. Allow yourself to be aware of how good it feels to be relaxed and to be at peace.

Every time that you listen to this healing tape, you will relax more deeply than the time before. Each time you listen to this recording, you will relax more deeply and completely than the time before.

Use your good imagination, (*your name*), and see a beautiful white light. White light is the symbol for God's Love. Imagine this beautiful white light shining through the sky, and shining into the top of your head now. Feel the white light in your brain. See it illuminating every cell of your mind with God's perfect Love. God's Love is healing your brain now. Healing your thoughts so that all of your thoughts are positive. You expect to live a long and healthy life. All of your thoughts about the future are happy thoughts. Your thoughts about yourself are always loving and kind. You like yourself. It is healthy to love yourself. You love yourself now.

The white light in your mind has infinite intelligence within it. The infinite intelligence of God is filling your brain with divine intelligence. You are intelligent, (*your name*). Every part of your body is controlled by your mind. The white light is healing every cell and every nerve in your brain. Your mind is clear.

Feel the beautiful, loving light filling your entire head with divine love. Unconditional love. God loves you dearly. God's Love is healing your eyes now. You see clearly and perfectly. Your ears are filled with the white light of God's Love and you hear perfectly now. God's Love is balancing, harmonizing and healing every cell of your nose and your sinuses. You breathe easily now. Your mouth and teeth and gums are filled with divine love and light. God's Love is healing your head now. See the light of God's Love pouring into your neck. Your neck is healthy and flexible and strong. Feel the light pouring into your shoulders. Your shoulders are relaxed and healthy now.

The healing white light of God's Love is streaming into every cell of your arms and hands. God's Love is healing your body now. Your arms are healthy. Your hands are flexible and healthy.

Feel the loving, healing light in your back and spine. Your back is relaxed now. Your back is flexible and strong. Every vertebra of your spine is being rejuvenated now. Your back is healthy and well.

Imagine and feel the white light pouring into your chest, (*your name*). Take a deep breath and fill your lungs with God's healing Love now. Feel the presence of God's Love in your heart. See the healing light in your heart. Your heart is healthy and strong and full of love.

Feel God's Love and light pouring into your digestive system now. Your stomach, your liver, your pancreas and spleen are glowing with the healing light of God's perfect Love. Your intestines are healthy and normal. Your kidneys are functioning perfectly. See and feel the white light balancing and harmonizing every organ of your reproductive system. God's Love is rejuvenating your body now.

Imagine the white light of God's Love pouring into your legs now. Your legs are strong and healthy. Your feet are shining with the divine light now. Your feet are strong. Your understanding of life is growing stronger every day. You feel healthy. You have energy and pep. You have get up and go. Your entire body is becoming stronger and stronger every day now. The equalizing, harmonizing healing power of the Holy Spirit is established within you now and you are whole and well.

(*Speak your personal affirmation three times here.*)

_____

_____

_____

Your mind and body have accepted the idea of healing, and you are at peace.

When I count to the number five, you will open your eyes and feel good all over. You will feel better than you have felt in a long, long time.

Number one. Number two. Number three. Number four. Number five. Open your eyes and feel good. You feel great now.

APPENDIX C

SENDING GOD'S LOVE

When you start your day, sit in a quiet room, close your eyes and think, "God, I send Your perfect Love ahead of me into this day. I send Your Love into all of my thoughts, words and deeds. I send Your Love to everyone I will come in contact with today, in person, by mail, or on the phone. I send Your Love into every communication today. I fill this home to overflowing with Your divine Love so that all who enter here, myself included, will feel your loving Presence. I send Your Love to myself, to my body and into my relationships, my work and my finances. God, I send Your Love out to everyone in this city, this state, this country, and to everyone on earth. I send an extra abundance of Love to all the world leaders. I cover this planet with a huge cloud of God's Love and I send beams of Love to every man, woman and child on earth, leaving no one out."

Before you go to sleep, pray: "Dear God, I surround myself with your perfect Love. I am safe and protected. I send Your Love ahead of me into my sleep so that all of my dreams will be pleasant and I will sleep well tonight. I send Your Love out to everyone, everywhere. God, I send Your Love ahead of me into tomorrow. Amen."

APPENDIX D

PRAYER FOR A PARTNER

FOR A FEMALE PARTNER

Dear God,
Thank you for this beautiful day. Thank you for all the many blessings that you have given us in such great abundance. Thank you for this time of sharing with (your partner's name).

I invite your healing, holy spirit into this time and into this relationship.

I ask that you bless _____ abundantly. I ask that you heal her in every way that she may need, physically, mentally, emotionally, and spiritually.

I ask that you fill her mind with your divine peace. And fill her heart with your perfect love. Fill every cell of her body with your healing, balancing, rejuvenating, life energy, so that every cell and every part of her body is healthy, and well. I especially ask that you heal her _____. Restore her body to health and her mind to peace.

We are touching in agreement on this, and we give thanks that you always answer our prayers. And so it is. Amen.

FOR A MALE PARTNER

Dear God,
Thank you for this beautiful day. Thank you for all the many blessings that you have given us in such great abundance. Thank you for this time of sharing with (your partner's name).

I invite your healing, holy spirit into this time and into this relationship.

I ask that you bless _____ abundantly. I ask that you heal him in every way that he may need, physically, mentally, emotionally, and spiritually.

I ask that you fill his mind with your divine peace. And fill his heart with your perfect love. Fill every cell of his body with your healing, balancing, rejuvenating, life energy, so that every cell and every part of his body is healthy, and well. I especially ask that you heal his_____. Restore his body to health and his mind to peace.

We are touching in agreement on this, and we give thanks that you always answer our prayers. And so it is. Amen.

APPENDIX E

AFFIRMATION OF THE WEEK

Cut the following affirmations from this book and place them where you will see them often. If you have borrowed this book from a library or a friend, photocopy these affirmations.

WEEK 1

> ## I LOVE AND APPRECIATE MYSELF

WEEK 2

> ## I AM RELAXED

WEEK 3

I AM LISTENING TO MY BODY NOW

WEEK 4

I NOW FORGIVE EVERYONE AND EVERYTHING THAT MAY NEED FORGIVING, INCLUDING MYSELF

WEEK 5

I LET GO OF EVERYTHING AND EVERYONE THAT IS NO LONGER FOR MY HIGHEST GOOD

WEEK 6

I COMMUNICATE CLEARLY, EFFECTIVELY, AND HONESTLY NOW

RECOMMENDED READING

Love, Medicine and Miracles
by Bernie Siegel

The Dragon Doesn't Live Here Anymore
by Alan Cohen

Self Hypnosis and Beyond
by Don Weldon

Healing Words
by Larry Dossey, M.D.

Loving Relationships
by Sondra Ray

Songs of the Night
by Gian Michael Salvato

You Can Heal Your Life
by Louise Hay

A Return to Love
by Marianne Williamson

Teach Only Love
by Gerald G. Jampolsky, M.D.

Healing Secrets of the Ages
by Catherine Ponder

ABOUT THE AUTHOR

Joanna Rose Light is a spiritual teacher and healer. She has been teaching universal prayer principles to groups and individuals since 1978. Through her tapes, seminars and personal counseling she has helped thousands of people to heal their bodies and enrich their lives.

Joanna is available for lectures and seminars anywhere and makes every effort to respond to all requests. If you would like to sponsor such an event please write for more information.

THE PERFECT GIFT!

Order this book
"PRAYER THE REMEDY THAT ALWAYS WORKS"
for your family and friends.

$12.95 each

Call toll free 1-800-319-9572 or see order form on last page.

TAPES by Joanna Rose Light - These tapes all have original, relaxing music in the background. Complete instructions are included.

GOD WILL HEAL YOUR BODY

*Combines prayer and relaxation to heal body and soul

*Awaken your spiritual energies

*This is the tape that goes with this book

ACCELERATED HEALING

*Speed up the healing process

*Leave your problems in the past

*Feel as if you have taken a long relaxing vacation

SELF -CONFIDENCE

*Feel comfortable with others

*Make decisions with assurance

*Increase your self-esteem

SLEEP WELL TONIGHT

*Fall asleep naturally

*Have pleasant dreams

*Feel refreshed tomorrow

RELEASE POUNDS
*Feel satisfied with less food (Eat less and feel better)
*Reduce weight and add years to your life
*Look and feel thinner, better and more attractive

MONEY RICH
*Increase your income
*Manage money wisely
*Create financial security

ATTRACT YOUR PERFECT MATE
*Feel and become more attractive
*Meet a compatible mate
*Build a rewarding and lasting relationship

SEXUAL FULFILLMENT
*Enhance the pleasure and intimacy of sex
*Increase sexual desire and frequency
*Add new life to your relationship

EASY CHILDBIRTH
*Learn to relax your body
*Have a painless delivery
*Enjoy a happy pregnancy

IMPROVE YOUR MEMORY
*Remember names, dates, facts and numbers
*Recall information quickly and easily
*Increase your self-confidence

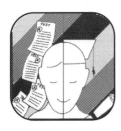

PASS EXAMS
*Become motivated to study
*Trust your memory
*Learn the secret of passing tests
Every student should have this tape.

STOP SMOKING FOREVER
*No weight gain and no cravings
*Enjoy better health and longer life
*A three tape set

ORDER FORM

<u>BOOK</u>: Prayer, The Remedy That Always Works..........$12.95X ___ = _____

<u>TAPES</u>: **$10.95 each or 3 for $25.**

     GOD WILL HEAL YOUR BODY............................$10.95 X ___ = _____

     ACCELERATED HEALING..$10.95 X ___.=_____

     SELF CONFIDENCE...$10.95 X ___ = _____

     SLEEP WELL TONIGHT..$10.95 X ___ = _____

     RELEASE POUNDS...$10.95 X ___ = _____

     MONEY RICH..$10.95 X ___ = _____

     ATTRACT YOUR PERFECT MATE.............................$10.95 X ___ =_____

     SEXUAL FULFILLMENT...$10.95 X ___ = _____

     EASY CHILDBIRTH...$10.95 X ___ = _____

     IMPROVE YOUR MEMORY..$10.95 X ___ = _____

     PASS EXAMS..$10.95 X ___ = _____

     STOP SMOKING FOREVER........3 tapes.......................$25.00 X ___ = _____

                                       Subtotal _____

                   Arizona Residents Add 7.25% Taxes _____

                               Shipping $3<u>.00</u>

                                Total $_____

Your Name _____

Street   _____

City   _____ _____ State _____ Zip _____

Area Code _____ Phone _____

Visa___ MC___ Acct #_____Expires_____

Signature_____

Send check or money order to:
Peace of Mind Publishing, P.O. Box 10354, Phoenix, AZ 85064

Phone orders, call (602) 212-1312 or fax orders, call (602) 212-1152

Special Order Hotline 1-800-319-9572